Elizabeth Ann Seton

Saint for a New Nation

ELIZABETH ANN SETON

SAINT FOR A NEW NATION

by Julie Walters

PAULIST PRESS
New York/Mahwah, N.J.

Cover art and interior illustrations by Patrick Kelley

Cover design by Lynn Else

Text copyright © 2002 by Julie Walters
Illustrations © 2002 by Patrick Kelley

Library of Congress Cataloging-in-Publication Data

Walters, Julie.
    Elizabeth Ann Seton : saint for a new nation / by Julie Walters.
      p.   cm.
    Includes bibliographical references.
    ISBN 0-8091-6692-5
    1. Seton, Elizabeth Ann, Saint, 1774–1821. 2. Christian saints—United States—Biography. 3. Daughters of Charity of St. Vincent de Paul—United States—Biography. I. Title.

BX4700.S4 .W35 2001
271'.9102—dc21
[B]
                                         2001055188

Published by Paulist Press
997 Macarthur Boulevard
Mahwah, New Jersey 07430

www.paulistpress.com

Printed and bound in the
United States of America

CONTENTS

Author's Note.   vii

Chapter One.   There's No Need to Cry   1

Chapter Two.   At Home on Uncle Bayley's Farm   8

Chapter Three.   My Dearest Will   16

Chapter Four.   I Have Become a Looker Up   24

Chapter Five.   My World Is My Family   35

Chapter Six.   Thy Will Be Done   41

Chapter Seven.   Bless Me with Faith   51

Chapter Eight.   On God Himself I Pin My Faith   61

Chapter Nine.   I Am a Catholic   71

Chapter Ten.   The Sweetest Dream
                    of My Imagination   82

Chapter Eleven.   A Grain of Seed for Eternal Life   89

Chapter Twelve.   Troubled on Every Side   97

Chapter Thirteen.   Preparing Good Leaven   105

Chapter Fourteen.   The Little Mustard Seed   110

Chapter Fifteen.   Roar from the Valley   118

Epilogue.   127

Notes.   129

Selected Bibliography.   133

Author's Note

This book is meant to provide an understanding of Elizabeth Seton's life and the events that shaped her character and spirituality. Her story is presented as a narrative, and dialogue is used to maintain continuity, reader interest, and dramatic pace. Though there are no footnotes within this narrative, dialogue and thoughts are quoted or paraphrased from historical sources or from the journals and lively correspondence Mother Seton maintained throughout her life. Mother Seton's actual writings are the copyrighted property of the individual repositories in which they are archived. Her writings tapped for this book are used with permission, courtesy of the archives, Daughters of Charity, Emmitsburg, Pennsylvania.

Phrases such as "My darling little girl," "Dear Little Sharer of my Lot," and many religious expressions used by Elizabeth Seton and others throughout the book should be seen as the normal language of the period, one that's over two hundred years removed from ours. These expressions should not be interpreted to mean that Elizabeth was affected, overly sweet, or docile. Behind the deceptively sweet language stands a tough-minded woman who faced an unbelievably difficult life with immense strength, purpose, and character.

Acknowledgments and Dedication

Many heartfelt thanks to Sister Betty Ann McNeil, D.C., archivist of St. Joseph's Provincial House, Emmitsburg, Maryland; to Sister Aloysia Dugan, D.C., former archivist of St. Joseph's Provincial House; to Bonnie Weatherly; to my dear friend, Tom Noe, who pointed me in the right direction when I was confused, and who spent hours reading and correcting many versions of this manuscript; to my editor, Susan O'Keefe, who with the patience of a midwife saw this project through to completion; and to Clem, friend husband, who has been an indefatigable booster who has loved me through hours and hours of research and writing, and to whom I dedicate this book.

CHAPTER ONE
THERE'S NO NEED TO CRY

Six-year-old Elizabeth Ann Bayley dashed up the steep stairs to the attic window, looked out, and dashed back down.

"The sun hasn't set yet, Emma," she said to her two-year-old half sister. She took Emma's chubby hand and, forcing herself to be patient, helped her up each step. Kneeling in front of the window, which reached almost to the floor, Elizabeth held Emma close and pointed to the setting sun. The large orange-red host, elevated above the naked trees, outlined the clouds below it in shades of purple and pink.

"I love to look at the sky and sunsets, Emma. It makes me feel close to my Mama. She died when I was about as old as you. Then Father brought your mama home to live with us." Elizabeth's voice became a whisper. "Then my baby sister died and not long after she died, you were born. Now you are my baby sister."

Elizabeth hugged her half sister closer. "When my baby sister died, I sat on the front porch looking up at the clouds, and our neighbor lady asked me why I wasn't crying. I told her, 'There's no need to cry. Little Kitty is in heaven with Mama.'" Elizabeth sighed. "I know Mama is happy with God, but I miss her all the same. I wish I could be with her."

ELIZABETH ANN SETON

Elizabeth felt sad inside, the same way she did when her Mama and her baby sister died. She remembered how she wanted to sit on her new mother's lap, to feel close to her, and to tell her how lost she felt. But Elizabeth's mother-in-law, as a stepmother was called in colonial days, was not the kind of woman who wanted to cuddle a little girl on her lap. Mrs. Bayley helped Elizabeth and her older sister Mary with their grooming and their dress, taught them social graces and their lessons, but she allowed them to call her only Mrs. Bayley, not Mama. She could never be called Mama by another woman's children.

"I miss Father, too, don't you? It's lonesome to be a child of a doctor. But a doctor is needed during wartime, Emma. We must be brave. Father is brave. He's helping all the soldiers wounded in the conflict."

Elizabeth talked on, as if Emma understood about war and gunshots, houses burning, and British Red Coats in the streets.

One year before the Revolutionary War, before the birth of the United States of America, when the United States was still thirteen British colonies, Elizabeth Ann Bayley was born in the general area of New York City. It was August 28, 1774. New York was then one of the largest ports in the British colonies. The harbor teemed with British ships, and the colonies were filled with resentment against English laws benefiting the mother country while penalizing them. Some men, disguised as Indians, threw a cargo of tea into Boston Harbor, a clear signal that the colonies were finished with unfair English laws. Later, people called it the Boston Tea Party.

A month after Elizabeth's birth, delegates from twelve colonies met in Philadelphia. In a bold step, the First

Continental Congress decided that the colonies should take up arms against England. A year later, in April, 1775, the American Revolutionary War began. English forces occupied New York. On July 4, 1776, the Declaration of Independence proclaimed that America was a single, separate people and the united colonies a separate nation.

When war broke out, Elizabeth's father, Dr. Richard Bayley, was in England mastering the latest surgical and medical skills. Although loyal to Great Britain, he was desperate to return to his wife, Catherine, and their two little daughters, Mary and Elizabeth. He boarded the first ship to America, a British warship. But shortly after his return his wife died in childbirth. The thirty-three-year-old doctor soon realized that Mary, Elizabeth, and baby Kitty needed a mother, and a year later he married nineteen-year-old Charlotte Amelia Barclay, the daughter of Andrew and Helena Roosevelt Barclay. Then Kitty died and the new Mrs. Bayley had a child of her own. She named the baby for herself, but called her Emma.

"Emma, let's pray." Turning Emma's face toward her own, Elizabeth said, "We will pray that the war will end, all the British soldiers will leave, and Father can come home to us. I'll teach you the Our Father. Look at my mouth, Emma, and say after me, 'Our Father.'"

"Faver," repeated Emma.

"Who art in heaven," coached Elizabeth.

"Heben," said Emma.

Elizabeth smiled her encouragement. When they finished, sun and clouds were gone; trees stood like black sentinels against a lavender sky. Elizabeth listened to the noises in the house. After-dinner clatter had softened to murmuring bedtime preparations. Elizabeth could hear Mary helping Mrs. Bayley.

"Come, Emma, time for bed." Elizabeth covered her sister's chubby hand with her own and carefully helped her down the steps.

While Mrs. Bayley put Emma to bed, Mary worked on her sums and Elizabeth practiced her marking, as printing was called then. She copied Psalm 23 from the big Bible on the table in front of her. Mrs. Bayley was teaching her the psalm; printing it helped Elizabeth learn.

"Mary," Elizabeth whispered, "our poor mother-in-law is in great affliction. This morning our neighbor said the British were going to cut off our food and fuel."

"She's just tired, Bet, because of another baby inside her. Her relatives, the Roosevelts, are wealthy and will see that she gets what she needs." At age ten, Mary was already practical.

Mrs. Bayley sat down wearily on her chair at the table, her head against folded hands. They could hear the sounds of distant gunfire. "We must have courage," she said. "The Lord will take care of us. Let's pray the twenty-third psalm together. You remember it, don't you, Elizabeth?"

Elizabeth nodded. She said this psalm when she missed her father. They prayed softly together.

> *The Lord is my shepherd,*
> *I shall not want.*
> *He makes me to lie down in green pastures.*
> *He leads me beside still waters;*
> *He refreshes my soul.*
> *He leads me in paths of righteousness*
> *For his name's sake.*

When they finished praying, Mrs. Bayley, holding a candle overhead, led Elizabeth and Mary to the bedroom. Elizabeth watched the candlelight's shadows on the wall and prayed to herself: *Though I walk in the midst of the shadow of death I will fear no evil, for thou art with me.* She climbed into bed next to Mary, pulling the covers over her head. *Thou prepare a table before me in the presence of my enemies.* Bursts of light followed by loud explosions like thunder lit up the dark room. *Surely goodness and kindness shall follow me all the days of my life. And I shall dwell in the house of the Lord forever.* Elizabeth put her hands over her ears. *But Lord,* she ended, *could Father not come home soon?*

Though blackened and bloodied, the colonies fought on until they were victorious, and independence was won. In 1781, the first government was approved, giving birth to the United States of America. But it was not until 1783 that British forces left New York and the city began to rebuild. Fires had destroyed much of the city, including Trinity Episcopal Church where Elizabeth perhaps had been baptized.

The Episcopal Church was the church of the wealthy aristocracy of New York City: lawyers, independent landowners, merchants, elected and appointed government officials, and eminent physicians. Dr. Bayley, one of the first health officers of the port of New York, was in this distinguished class, but he thought service to his fellow man could replace church attendance.

New York buzzed with gossip about the controversial physician. Some hailed him as the most dedicated doctor in New York, saying he was tender and compassionate to both rich and poor. They told stories of his jumping from his horse, tending a soldier who had been run down and left lying in the street, then being thrown into prison himself by the British government because the soldier was a patriot. They also spoke of how his research found a cure for croup, saving the lives of countless children.

Others said he was proud and that he neglected his family for his medical practice. They said his temper flared when New York City officials opposed as too costly his plan to rid the city of yellow fever by filling in the swamps and by getting rid of the filth in the streets and around the docks. When he fought the city officials in the state legislature, they said it was the height of arrogance.

And still others said that Dr. Bayley married the second Mrs. Bayley only so that she could care for his girls and he could continue his medical pursuits. When the gossip reached Mrs. Bayley's ears she began to imagine that Dr. Bayley preferred Elizabeth and Mary to her own children, and that she must do something about such partiality—but what?

More evidence of Dr. Bayley's favoritism seemed to lie in his decision that Elizabeth and Mary be enrolled in a private school run by a woman known as Mama Pampelion. However, he merely hoped it would relieve Mrs. Bayley of his girls during the day. Besides, such schooling was in keeping with their social position as a prominent New York family. Mama Pampelion would teach his girls French, needlework, drawing, music, and the social graces, in addition to the three Rs.

One day while ten-year-old Elizabeth was at the school, she was unable to concentrate on her French lesson. Looking out the window she saw her father, medical bag in hand, getting out of his carriage. She was proud that her father was one of the first doctors to make house calls by carriage. Mama Pampelion was busy helping another student, so Elizabeth slipped out of her seat and tiptoed quietly across the room and out the door. She saw her father so little, she was sure Mama Pampelion would understand. Chestnut curls dancing, Elizabeth ran after her father.

"Betty! Is today a free day?" Dr. Bayley's face was first surprised, then stern.

Elizabeth hugged her father's neck, then kissed his cheek. "No, Father, I saw you out the window and wanted to give you a kiss."

"And what about your studies? You were not paying attention?"

"Oh, Father, French is so tiresome. It makes my head ache. Besides, I'll never go to France."

Dr. Bayley stooped down and kissed the top of Elizabeth's head. "Sauciness does not become you, Bet," he admonished, with a hint of humor in his voice. He loved his spirited daughter, but his duty was to encourage the studies she liked the least—French and the piano.

"Heed my words, Betty. French and music must each have their hours. I'll try to be home early tonight so you can play for me." He picked up his bag and hurried up the street.

"I've been practicing the German hymn for you," she called after him, but he didn't hear. Watching her father enter a doorway, she thought, *If I don't count on his being home, I won't be disappointed.* She walked back to her classroom and quietly slipped into her chair. *Maybe what people say is true. Maybe Father does love doctoring more than his family. More than me.*

CHAPTER TWO
AT HOME ON
UNCLE BAYLEY'S FARM

"Giddyap, Red."

Dr. Bayley flicked the reins to keep his sleek sorrel at a steady trot as he paced off the fifteen miles from New York to New Rochelle. He was taking Elizabeth and Mary to stay with his younger brother, William, whom the girls called Uncle Bayley, for the two years he'd be in England pursuing his medical studies. Dr. Bayley talked excitedly about his research, but fourteen-year-old Elizabeth couldn't share his enthusiasm.

Why is Mrs. Bayley sending us away again? she thought. *I understand how having six children in eight years has been hard on her, but surely Mary and I are a great help. She knows we like doing household chores and caring for the babies. Yet she acts as if Mary and I are the burden. Nothing we do seems to please her anymore. She always seems angry with us. Still, I would rather be home than sent away like this — and for two years!*

Even so, Elizabeth loved the 250-acre farm with its woods and the waters of Long Island Sound just down the hill from it. The large friendly clapboard farmhouse was always filled with cousins and friends. She was happy when she had stayed there before while her father was in England, when she was eight and again at twelve. And she loved Uncle Bayley. He was like her favorite rock on the beach—it was always there, and so was he. He encouraged her to read the books in his library and afterwards talked to her about them. He was so kind to her and Mary, kind to his neighbors and the townsfolk. He even treated his servants like family.

His wife Elizabeth's Aunt Sarah also looked on Elizabeth and Mary as her own children. Her arms were always open wide in welcome. She seemed to be everywhere at once, caring for each person's comfort.

Let's see, Elizabeth thought, trying to cheer herself up so she wouldn't cry. *How old are my four cousins now? William must be 16, Joseph is 11, Richard is 9, and Ann would be 6. Suzanne is 14, like me. What fun we will have passing ourselves off as sisters because we both look so French!*

Her mind then skipped to unmarried Aunt Molly Besley, who tutored the cousins in French. Whose side she was related to Elizabeth could never figure out, but it didn't matter. She loved to sit at Aunt Molly's feet for hours during large family gatherings and chat about God, scripture, and prayer.

Elizabeth remembered her other visits to the farm. While she liked her relatives, she had also liked the hours she spent alone by the seashore humming favorite hymns, playing tag with the surf, collecting shells. Every rock, bird, insect, leaf, floating cloud, and wide expanse of water seemed to be God's footprints, directing her thoughts to heaven.

The carriage pulled up to the farmhouse. Relatives, friends, and welcoming shouts poured from it like fresh lemonade from a pitcher.

Elizabeth stepped from the carriage and was engulfed by a wave of love and warmth. Uncles, aunts, and cousins welcomed her and her sister with hugs and handshakes.

Elizabeth giggled and curtsied when Uncle Bayley bowed like an English squire. He kissed her hand, then hugged her tight. "'Tis a blessing you will be with us for a while, Bet."

Aunt Sarah wrapped her in her arms. "My, you've grown into a pretty young lady these last two years."

Elizabeth climbed the porch steps and kissed Aunt Molly B.'s soft cheek.

"Welcome, little friend," Aunt Molly said in French.

"Merci," Elizabeth answered.

Everyone laughed and talked at once until, above the din, Uncle Bayley hollered, "Your Aunt Sarah has refreshments for us out under the trees."

The excitement buried Elizabeth's feelings of abandonment until she heard her father's lowered voice. *He's beginning his goodbyes,* she thought. She excused herself and threaded her way to her father, who put his arm around her shoulder. Fighting tears, she kissed him goodbye, saying cheerily but with a leaden heart, "Two years will go by quickly."

Aunt Sarah slipped one arm around her and the other around Mary. Trying not to feel so forsaken, Elizabeth wondered, *Why do I have to experience everything so keenly? Why can't I take things as they come, as Mary does?*

Despite her loneliness for her father, Elizabeth felt truly at home on Uncle Bayley's farm. Spring yielded to summer, and she was quickly immersed in the farm's bustling warmth. She sailed the Sound with her cousin William, licking sea spray from her face. She galloped the fields with her cousin Suzanne and relished quiet beach walks. She skipped flat stones across the purple water and sat on her favorite rock to watch the pink glow of sunset. The glorious colors were ever a reminder of her mother and of the God who created it all, with whom she would one day share the loveliness of heaven. Yet she always asked herself, *I wonder what Father is doing right now?*

According to her father's advice, Elizabeth kept her hours for music and joined her cousins for French lessons with Aunt Molly B. She set times for morning and evening prayer from the Book of Common Prayer, for Bible reading, for memorization of the psalms, for study, and for serious reading. To please her father she kept a journal, writing down thoughts, prayers, and passages from scripture, poems, and books.

Elizabeth also joined her relatives, part of the town's gentry, for New Rochelle's social gatherings. She was a favorite at dinner parties. Well-read and educated, she delighted her French relatives by sprinkling her conversation with French phrases. She accepted invitations to play the piano because it brought the guests such obvious joy. And on the dance floor, at barely five feet tall, she looked like a porcelain doll. Her chestnut curls framed her oval face, enhanced her large black eyes, and bounced with every step.

One night, while sipping a cup of punch, she overheard a relative complimenting her many fine attributes.

Agreeing, another woman added, "The young people love her too. She makes everything fun for...."

Without waiting to hear the rest, Elizabeth walked away, thinking, *I am much too pleased by what I have just heard. I must guard myself from vanity.*

Summer's hot muggy days dwindled, then cool evenings and haze above the woods heralded autumn's advance. Gold wheatfields and sun-faded cornfields awaited the reapers' scythes. Elizabeth and Aunt Molly B. would refresh themselves in the evening's coolness. Silhouetted against the blue-gray twilight, heads bent toward one another as they conspired to do good deeds together—visits to the sick or sorrowful—their conversations now and then erupted in muffled laughter. Elizabeth began to glimpse the soul's deep contentment in serving others.

Autumn came. Fields and woods wore every tint and shade of red and yellow. Wheat sheaves stood bright gold against the blue, blue sky. Geese winged south in wide Vs. Fruits, vegetables, and grain were gathered in and stored. Shorter days, longer nights, dark clouds, and chilling rains grayed the countryside—a dreary world to Elizabeth who in all these months had not received one letter from her father nor any news of him.

One morning she awoke to frosted trees and snowy fields, a bleak white desert which mirrored her aching heart. Neither winter's ice skating, nor sledding parties, nor a book of pious essays read while toasting by the fire could melt her icy fear that her father cared nothing about her, or perhaps was even dead.

After weeks of gloom and still no letter, she determined to conquer her mood. She bundled up and walked out to the Sound, singing hymns. The wind bit her cheeks. All was frozen white except the slate-colored sea. She brushed snow from her rock, her favorite place to be alone, and climbed onto it.

Standing on the rock, Elizabeth began to shout verses of Psalm 18.

"The Lord is my rock, my fortress, my deliverer!" she shouted through broken sobs and tears. "My God in whom I take refuge! My stronghold! I call upon the Lord, who is worthy to be praised, and I am saved from my enemies!"

Her loneliness, like winter's ice in springtime, began to melt. *God* was her Father, faithful and true! *He* would not forsake her. Uncle William, Aunt Sarah, and all her cousins loved her as well—and dear Aunt Molly, who always knew how to look at things.

One morning a few months later, in spring of 1789, before Elizabeth even opened her eyes, she thought, *My Father doesn't love me. I have not heard from him for a year. If he loved me, he would write to me. But perhaps he cannot write. Perhaps he is ill. Or dead.* Tears stung her eyes. She opened them. Her bedroom window framed a bright blue sky.

"I cannot let my imagination rule me," she said aloud. "I have to get hold of myself. If Father doesn't love me, if he is dead, and if my stepmother Mrs. Bayley doesn't want me, I have a home here with people who *do* love me."

She jumped out of bed, opened the window to the fragrant spring air, then saw her cousin Joseph hitching the horses to the wood cart. Waving, she called, "Wait for me."

She dressed, ran down the stairs and through the kitchen, snatched a biscuit, ran across the lawn, and hopped on the back of the cart. Munching her biscuit, she quoted aloud from the poetry collection titled *The Seasons* by James Thomson, which she had grabbed on her way out:

> *Still let my song a nobler note assume,*
> *And sing th' infusive force of Spring on man.*
> *When heaven and earth, as if contending, vie*
> *To raise his being and serene his soul,*
> *Can he forbear to join the general smile*
> *Of nature? Can fierce passions vex his breast,*
> *While every gale is peace, and every grove*
> *Is melody?*

ELIZABETH ANN SETON

A mile from the house Elizabeth hopped from the cart and set off through the wood. Stepping over a fallen moss-covered tree, she gathered a handful of dark blue violets, ducked under a limb, added white snowdrops. She held back a branch to allow herself to pass, stopped, tilted her head back, and breathed in the smell of moist earth. She knelt down to gather yellow cowslips and ferns, growing like green feathers at the base of a tree, and looked up into the clear blue vault of sky overhead.

"O Lord, our Lord, how majestic is thy name in all the earth." The words of Psalm 8 leapt from her lips.

So full of love for God she could not speak, Elizabeth looked around for a place to sit. Walking over to a chestnut tree with saplings growing around, she sat down on a bed of moss and said aloud, "A fine green mattress indeed."

Nose buried in her sweet bouquet, she lay quietly gazing at the sky and listening to the lark and jenny wren.

"O God, you are my Father," she whispered. "Perhaps my father does not love me. Perhaps he is dead. But you love me. I have so many proofs of your love and care all around me—not only in the work of your hands, but in the kindness of my relations and friends. O God, you will care for me no matter what happens. You are my Father, my all."

Speech, thoughts, understanding were silenced. Sky, trees, sun receded. Her spirit adored and loved her God. Ever so quietly and gently, God the Father's love filled her soul with deep peace and certain knowledge of his constant care and love. She passed two hours in tears, laughter, hymns, prayer, deep heavenly peace.

On the farm the seasons made their rounds again—planting, growing, harvesting—with still no word from Dr. Bayley. When he at last returned to the United States and to Uncle Bayley's farm, he brought disturbing news of a bitter quarrel with his wife.

"There has been a family disagreement between Mrs. Bayley and myself," he told Elizabeth and Mary. Elizabeth saw how her father spoke through clenched teeth, trying to control his anger. "I will take up residence separate from her. You and Mary will continue to stay here with your Uncle Will and Aunt Sarah."

"We are no longer welcome in our own home?" Mary asked.

"That is right." Dr. Bayley's eyes were dark with fury.

"Is there no hope of reconciliation?" asked Elizabeth.

"Never," her father said with finality.

Elizabeth fought back tears, thinking, *What can have happened to cause such a disagreement? Why won't Father tell us? Could it be over Mary and me? Will I never have a home again?*

CHAPTER THREE
MY DEAREST WILL

At New Rochelle, Elizabeth matured like wheat under the summer sun. She had left home a child and was now a beautiful, poised, confident sixteen-year-old who slipped easily into New York's elite social circle and their continuous round of teas, dinner parties, and balls. At the same time she felt confused and isolated. Even though she had grown closer to her father since his return from England, and even though they corresponded almost daily, he still would not talk about his quarrel with Mrs. Bayley. Elizabeth tried to talk to her sister about it, but Mary was preoccupied. Dr. Wright Post, Dr. Bayley's medical student, had been calling on her in New Rochelle. Wedding preparations began in earnest, and Mary became Mrs. Post in June of 1790.

Once the newlyweds had established themselves, Elizabeth alternated between the Post home in Manhattan and the Long Island home of her Aunt Mary, her late mother's sister. Over the next four years, where Elizabeth lived at any moment depended on her aunt's circumstances, or whether her sister was confined with child. Elizabeth knew that both Aunt Mary and the Posts wanted her to feel welcome, but she felt awkward and displaced. She felt she could not be hostess to her friends in either place, so she often stayed in her room with her Bible, books, and journal. Among her few possessions she could pretend to have a home.

But the pretense did little to lift her mood. In her journal she wrote that she was subject to melancholy and that she preferred it to cheerfulness. Cheerfulness, she reasoned, might only be the result of a good night's sleep and could easily change to sadness while, if sadness changed, it would be to cheerfulness.

Her words prompted her to wonder if she were becoming too introspective. She had begun her journal to please her father, so she decided to ask him. Although he could not provide a home for her, he did provide guidance in his letters. Replying the next day, he wrote that a journal was like corresponding with one's self and so was a bit self-centered. Still, he allowed that she could continue her journal if she used it also as a way to learn new information.

Elizabeth kissed the letter before she put it in a box where she saved her correspondence. *What wisdom Father has for me,* she thought. *He **is** a good man, so dedicated to his patients, serving the poor and directing the New York Dispensary. Why will he not work as diligently to put an end to the family disagreement? How can anyone be an enemy to another?*

Tears burned her eyes as she remembered how kindly she had spoken to her half brothers and sisters during a recent social gathering and how they had turned and walked away without a word. She could still feel the hot embarrassed flush of being humiliated in front of her friends. The haughtiness of her half sister Emma had hurt the most.

Elizabeth threw herself across the bed. *If I've done something wrong, why doesn't someone tell me? I'd gladly ask forgiveness,* she thought. *Does not our pastor exhort us to be reconciled, to ask forgiveness for injuries and wrongs, and to be ready to forgive if another has offended us?* Elizabeth began to sob. *How can I be reconciled if I don't know what I've done? How could Mrs. Bayley not want me to live at home?* Elizabeth wished there were places in America, like in novels, where she could shut herself away from the world and all its miserable relationships, a place where she could simply pray and always be good.

Mary called through the door, "Elizabeth, time to leave for the dressmakers."

"Coming!"

Elizabeth jumped up, poured water from a pitcher into a basin, splashed her face, dried it, and fixed her hair. Changing clothes, she thought, *What a vexation balls are! So much time shopping for material, looking for matching slippers, getting endless fittings. I wish I could disguise myself as a working girl, stow away on a ship to Europe, and work for a living like the girls I've read of in books. Oh, but I do love the dancing,* she admitted as she buttoned up her dress. *And the pleasant company.*

The morning after a ball at the Sitgreaves, Elizabeth sat at her bedroom window reading the scriptures for the day and thanking God for his goodness and the previous evening's cheerfulness. William Magee Seton had filled most of her dance card. She remembered how kind, how tender, he was. How well-mannered, sincere, and dignified. How his brown eyes, serious one moment, had flashed with merriment the next. His father, the elder William Seton, was a director of the newly-formed Bank of New York and no doubt hoped that William Magee, the oldest son of his thirteen children, would follow in his footsteps.

As William and Elizabeth had danced last night, he told her about attending school in England for six years, about serving an apprenticeship under Filippo and Antonio Filicchi, his father's business connection in Italy, and about touring Europe which, his father said, would round out his education. William also told her how he had brought the first Stradivarius violin to the United States and how he'd once thought of playing as a profession, but his father had convinced him to learn a practical trade. William expounded on his love of opera in Florence, Italy, and how he found London quite gay, not dissipated like New York. Just last week he'd had to admonish his brother for gambling. "It's one of the worst vices of man," William said. "One cannot tell where it will lead if it becomes a habit."

Elizabeth loved his liveliness and admired his righteousness and honesty. She thought they must be natural virtues rather than from practicing one's religion. Her very close friend, Julia Sitgreaves Scott, told her that, like Dr. Bayley, William claimed allegiance to the Episcopal Church but did not attend. Julia also said William had written home from Europe about breathing problems. The family feared that, at twenty-two, he had the initial symptoms of tuberculosis, which the Setons called "the Seton Complaint" because it had claimed the lives of so many family members.

As they finished the last dance William had said, smiling down at her, "I'll be playing my violin at Mrs. Sadler's on Thursday next. I would like to ask her to invite you, if you're free."

Elizabeth's Bible crashed to the floor, startling her out of her reverie. *Oh, why can't I say my prayers and have good thoughts of God after an evening in public places,* she scolded herself. *I must not waste my time daydreaming.*

At that moment Mary rushed into Elizabeth's room.

"I have just heard the reason for our Father's separation from Mrs. Bayley," Mary said. "Mrs. Bayley has forced him to leave all his estate to her children. We are not even mentioned in his will!" With icy anger, Mary explained how their father, after a terrible quarrel with Mrs. Bayley, had signed over his entire estate to *her* children, leaving Elizabeth and Mary completely unprovided for. "Now I understand why Father says he will never be reconciled to her."

"Oh, Sister!" Elizabeth said, shocked. Conflicting emotions escaped in tears. She let Mary hold her close until she calmed herself and could think straight. "Mrs. Bayley always showed a preference for her own children while thinking Father loved you and me best. And she has been weakened by having so many children. She must fear that, if anything happened to her, Father would leave everything to us, and her children would be left with no inheritance. But Mary, how could she pressure Father into leaving us out completely?" Elizabeth took her sister's hand and tried to smile bravely. "Well, Father has always been more concerned with public service than with money. And you have married well. At least you are provided for now."

"You mustn't worry either," Mary said. "You have a home here for as long as you want. God has cared for us all these years." She added in a cheerier tone, "Perhaps young William Magee Seton is God's provision for you."

On Thursday evening at the Sadlers', Elizabeth watched William play the violin. She so loved his expression of concentration. When she looked up, Julia was staring at her with a knowing smile. Elizabeth felt herself blush.

William bowed graciously during the applause, then Elizabeth took a turn at the piano. She could feel William watching her and dared not look up at him. After the evening's entertainment they stood side by side, gratefully accepting thanks for their performances. Elizabeth flushed with pleasure when William whispered in her ear, "Let's find a cup of punch," and lightly touched her elbow to steer her to the refreshment table.

After that night William arranged many evenings for them together at the homes of mutual friends. They began seeing one another as often as they could and sent little notes back and forth, saying whose party they could be found at.

My dearest Will, Elizabeth might write, *If the weather remains clear, it is my intention to pass an hour with Mrs. Wilkes in the evening where you may have the honor of seeing me if you please. Your E.B.* Or on another occasion, *My dearest Will, If you are anxious to see your Eliza, you will find her at Mrs. Atkinsons' at the piano. Your own.*

In the months that followed, Elizabeth realized she and Will were one in mind and affections. She gave her heart completely to her dearest Will, whose ardent nature matched her own, and he in turn loved her intensely. It was not long before their courtship was the talk of New York.

One day Elizabeth confided to her sister, "Oh, Mary, I find myself beginning to think of a little country home where I can gather little children around and teach them to say their prayers and to be good."

Mary hugged Elizabeth, saying, "Father will be well pleased with his little Bet."

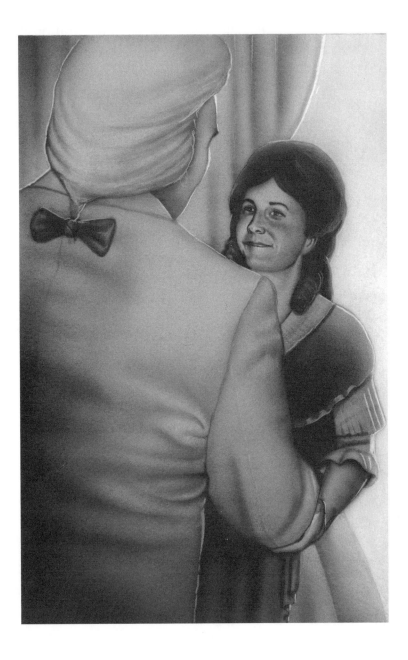

Heartened by Mary's assurance, Elizabeth encouraged William to talk with her father. William looked for an opportunity to ask the busy doctor for his permission. Not an easy task! But he persevered in his efforts to meet with Dr. Bayley. Finally, with the Doctor's blessing, Elizabeth and William were married on Sunday evening, January 25, 1794, in Wright and Mary Post's home. Elizabeth was nineteen years and five months, William was twenty-five.

CHAPTER FOUR
I HAVE BECOME A LOOKER UP

William brought Elizabeth to live in his father's house on Stone Street until theirs was ready. Like her own father, Mr. Seton had also married twice and had two sets of children, and it was this younger set of six who still lived with him. But unlike *her* step siblings, Will's spirited half brothers and sisters embraced Elizabeth as their own and she felt immediately at home, once again surrounded by children. At dinner, Rebecca, six years younger than Elizabeth, claimed the seat next to her. Charlotte, Mary, Harriet, and little Cecilia raced for their favorite places, while the elder Mr. Seton called his two youngest sons, Edward and Samuel, to stop their playful scuffling and sit on either side of their father. William seated Elizabeth next to himself, brushing her forehead with his lips. She smiled her love.

Mr. Seton refereed the joking and banter, then after dinner patted the little boys on the back. "A penny for the lad who can name all the Seton-Maitland ports," he said, referring to the family's new shipping business.

"London, Hamburg, Barcelona, Leghorn, and the West Indies," the boys recited rapidly in unison.

Mr. Seton tousled their hair. "Aha! Go fetch my strong box, Samuel. It's two pennies I'll gladly pay today." He turned to William. "I'm blessed indeed to have my oldest in this new shipping venture." He rose and clapped William Magee on the shoulder. "Let all come to my strong box while I'm alive and when I'm gone you will care for one another."

Sam brought the shiny black box to the table; Mr. Seton opened it, and the children helped themselves to a shiny coin.

Elizabeth's heart filled with love for her father-in-law. He was so generous and selfless, always up at daylight, the last to be in bed. And he used his wealth to help not only his beloved family, but also widows, orphans, and any others whose plight might reach his ears. She leaned over and whispered in her new husband's ear, "What a fine father Papa Seton is. I do love him, Will."

William smiled, pleased that Elizabeth saw his father's goodness. He covered her hand with his, squeezed it, then rose from his seat. "Father, excuse us. Elizabeth and I need to pack for my trip to Philadelphia tomorrow."

William's business trip was the first separation for the newly married couple. While Elizabeth folded William's shirts, she tucked a picture of herself between two of them to surprise him. The morning after he left, she wrote him two letters. A few days later came his reply, addressed to "My Darling Little Girl." Will wrote that it was Sunday but, rather than go to church, he was spending his time better by writing to his dear wife. He longed to return to her.

In October Elizabeth and William moved to 27 Wall Street, a few doors down from the Alexander Hamiltons. Elizabeth, filled with gratitude to God, looked out the window of her new home. *My own home at twenty! And a little one on the way,* she thought. *All this and heaven too!* She looked up into the skies. *If I dare to be so happy here on earth, will I be shut from heaven and lose you, Lord?*

In May, her fears about being too happy forgotten, she looked into newborn Anna Maria's large black eyes, so much like her own. Holding Anna close, Elizabeth said to her, "Now that I have a family all my own, I am completely happy. And your Grandfather Bayley's frequent visits only add to my joy." Still remembering the long separation from her father while she lived at New Rochelle, Elizabeth treasured their new closeness.

One night Dr. Bayley sank exhaustedly into a chair in the young Setons' parlor. "Just the sight of this little family refreshes me," he said to Elizabeth and William. He reached for Anna and bounced her on his knee. "My little Anna, there is more sense and intelligence in your rosy face than in any other in the world."

Anna's cheek dimpled.

"I declare that I can converse better with you than with any other woman in New York," Dr. Bayley laughed.

William picked up his violin. "A concert for the most sensible and intelligent woman in New York. And for her mother." He bowed to Elizabeth and played "Rosy Dimpled Boy," "Pauvre Madelon," "Return Enraptured Hours," and "Carmognol" as fast as his bow could sound them. Out of breath, he bowed before his ladies.

Elizabeth, hearing wheezing in his chest, lowered her head to keep William from seeing her fear. She prayed, *Dear God, I love Will more than anyone could love on earth. You, the Source of all love, must calm my fears.*

Elizabeth called for Mammy Huler, her trusted friend and servant. Forcing herself to sound calm and cheerful, Elizabeth said, "Anna has had the most pleasant conversation with her grandfather and the entertainment of her father's virtuoso violin and is now the most contented lady in New York. She asks only a good night's sleep."

Elizabeth took the sleepy child from Dr. Bayley, then held her for William to kiss. "Good night, my treasure." William kissed the baby's toes, hands, and forehead, then Elizabeth kissed her and handed her to Mammy, who carried her to the nursery, cooing and clicking her tongue.

Still hiding her fears, Elizabeth played her father's favorite songs as he stood next to the piano and sang. Afterward, while she wrote letters, William and her father played cribbage.

Elizabeth continued her correspondence long after Dr. Bayley left and Will had fallen asleep in his chair. As the clock struck ten, her fingers were stiff and cold and the candle was a stub. In a letter to her dear friend Julia, currently in Philadelphia, she revealed her fears about William's health. She concluded on a wistful note, in words as much about her separation from her friend as her fears for the future. She wrote that, at least in heaven, besides enjoying the bliss of being near the "Source of Perfection," loved ones could enjoy each other's company without the interruptions that came with life.

Not every evening found the Setons quietly at home. As leaders of New York's elite, they participated in social and civic functions and opened their home for dinner parties and evenings of music and entertainment. William was one of four men who hosted a gala ball honoring President Washington on his sixty-fifth birthday. And when St. John Theater opened in New York, the Setons were among its most faithful patrons.

Although these family and social duties kept her busy, Elizabeth was keenly aware of the suffering around her in the city. She joined with her sister-in-law, Rebecca, and several friends to establish the Society for the Relief of Poor Widows with Small Children. They collected food, clothing, and money to aid widows with no support.

The care of her own family increased when her first son, William, was born on November 24, 1796. As she nursed him one day, she pressed him close and said, "Dear Little Sharer of My Lot, I pray that you will stay innocent until you reach your heavenly home and never allow the pleasures of the world to lure you from your path to the Father."

When Willy was a year old, dear Grandfather Seton fell on the ice while escorting a guest to his carriage. At first no one was alarmed, but then his pain continued and his condition worsened until he at last became bedridden. Dear Grandfather Seton died in the spring of 1798.

As Elizabeth watched the throng of 500 following the casket to the cemetery, she thought it was fitting that so many should honor this man who spent his life honoring others. With fervent determination, she raised her eyes to heaven and prayed, *Father, nothing in this world with all its pleasures combined would tempt me to be more than a passenger through life. I will possess this life only because, while I have it, I am a candidate for a better one.*

In the months following his father's death, William wrapped himself in grief. Elizabeth confided to Mammy, "Oh, Mammy, Mr. Will's lost his closest friend. I don't know how to console him." Elizabeth, who was expecting their third child by then, sat down heavily in a rocker in the nursery. "He's overwhelmed by the responsibilities of the shipping business and now by the possibility of his many younger half brothers and sisters living with us." Elizabeth watched her friend and servant adjust the new curtains.

"Mammy, I also can't imagine being mother to six more children. You know how I love my quiet family circle."

"You know the good Lord has things in hand," Mammy scolded.

Yes, Elizabeth thought. Still she was fatigued, up with Will till one and two in the morning, sorting through Mr. Seton's business and family papers. She had a pen in her hand at all times, it seemed, except to sleep.

"I'm not talking against the dead," Mammy said, moving to the next window, "but what was in Mr. Seton's mind, not leaving a will? Now it's up to you to figure out if there's enough money to feed and school the young Setons." Finishing the last window, she turned to her young mistress.

"He always said that we'd take care of one another after he died." Elizabeth remembered fondly the nights he opened his strongbox to the children. "Oh, Mammy, I am weary. But I must support Mr. Will. And you're right, of course. The dear Lord never forsakes those who trust in his mercy. I must resign myself to his bidding and lift my spirits so I in turn might lift my dearest Will's."

Elizabeth knew it was God's bidding that the six youngest Setons should stay together and live with them instead of being separated and going to various older married brothers and sisters. But the Wall Street home was too small, so Elizabeth and William decided to move into the Seton family home on Stone Street. The move was delayed, however, because of the imminent birth of Elizabeth's baby. Temporarily, William sent his brothers to a boarding school in Connecticut. His sisters went to their older married sister, Eliza Maitland, whose country home, Cragdon, was at Bloomingdale. During Elizabeth's confinement, Anna and Willy went to their Aunt Eliza's too.

ELIZABETH ANN SETON

When Elizabeth went into labor, she was exhausted from the late hours and lack of rest. Dr. Bayley could see she was so weak that she could hardly cooperate with her body. After her final exertion, she lay almost unconscious, but was aware enough to know there had been no cry from her infant. She raised her head to see her father bending over her baby, forcing his breath into the little lungs. He blew and blew until, after what seemed like hours, the infant cried. He handed the baby to his daughter. "You've a fine son, Betty."

Elizabeth gently kissed the little head. "We'll name him Richard Bayley," she whispered. "With Seton at the end he shall be all the dearer to me." She looked up at her father. "I wish Will could have been here." Will had planned his business trip so that he would be with her, but the baby had had a plan of his own.

Dr. Bayley patted her arm. "He'll be back here soon and will be happy to have another son. But now you need to rest and regain your strength while Anna and Willy are still away—although perhaps you and Will should join them at the Maitlands'. The yellow fever is like the plague this year."

Elizabeth and William usually spent the summers at the Maitland family home in the country or at the seashore to escape the heat and the threat of yellow fever, but this summer William was chained to the business. He could not leave the city, and Elizabeth would not leave Will. Mary and Wright Post came down with a light case of fever and decided to go to the seashore as well. Mary tried to convince her sister to go with them, but Elizabeth refused. Even when a neighbor three doors away died of the fever, she would not relent.

One night Will sank wearily into a chair. Concerned, Elizabeth knelt at his feet. "Will, you're exhausted. Wouldn't it be best to take a weekend to see the children and rest? If you get worn down, you're more likely to get the fever."

Will thought a few minutes. "I think you're right. I miss the children and I am weary."

Elated, Elizabeth called, "Mammy, help me pack!"

The next day as they watched the children play on the beach, Elizabeth noticed Will's eyes were too bright. She jumped up and felt his head. He was burning up. *Oh Lord, she cried inside herself, my Will, my all, has yellow fever! What am I to do?* She forced herself to remain calm and said, "Will, I think you have yellow fever. I'll write to Father and ask him what to do."

She immediately went into the house and wrote to her father who was living at Bellevue Hospital in order to care for the many victims of the epidemic. Elizabeth called the houseboy and told him to bring her note to Doctor Bayley and to wait for an answer.

Doctor Bayley sent instructions and medicine, and Elizabeth nursed Will herself. Afterward she wrote to Julia that even though Will had just a light case of fever, she was able to persuade him to stay at the seashore until the cold weather. But that meant Will's half brothers and sisters would come and stay with them there and that there would be eighteen of them in five small rooms. Elizabeth wrote that she had become "A Looker Up," for her peace came only by looking up to God to supply it.

One morning, while they were still at the seashore, little Anna begged, "Ma, can we play in the garden?"

Willy, pulling at her skirt, objected in his baby talk, "No, Ma, can we go to the bread and butter closet?"

Young Sam Seton called from the door, "Sis, can I go down to the beach? Harriet will watch me."

Elizabeth, holding baby Richard, who would have nothing to do with Mammy, struggled to be patient with them all. "Yes, you can go to the beach, Sam. But wear a shirt," she said. Then turning to the Little Paddlers, as she called Anna and Willy, she said, "We'll find some bread and jam, then play in the garden."

When Elizabeth went out to the garden with the children, she found William sitting in a chair staring at the sea. He was weakened by the fever, still grieved by his father's death, worried about the business, and anxious about supporting so many in the house. Shaking his head dejectedly, he repeated over and over, "What shall become of us? The 'us' being so many."

Elizabeth kissed his head, praying, *O Dear Conductor of All Things, throw your veil of peace over us.*

They returned home to Wall Street in November. Elizabeth paused in the doorway, then walked slowly over to the piano. She caressed the smooth wood, sank to her knees, and laid her head against it, remembering happier carefree days when she played for William, her father, and gatherings of guests. Knowing she was soon to leave this home of her own, for which she'd waited so long, she wept.

Elizabeth, however, would not allow herself to be melancholy. There was too much to do. The Seton house on Stone Street had been the center of the yellow fever epidemic, so before the combined families moved in, William sold all the furnishings. Then Elizabeth, with faithful Mammy and a contingent of workmen at her side, papered, painted, whitewashed, and cleaned all the rooms, pantries, closets, storerooms, and cellars. A constant low fever from a boil under her arm, which Dr. Bayley lanced, could not deter Elizabeth from cleaning every corner to rid the house of germs. Then, united to God's will and with the thought, *I must draw near to Him who is my Comfort,* she left her Wall Street home.

CHAPTER FIVE

MY WORLD IS MY FAMILY

"It's good to have the older girls back," said Mammy. "And the two little boys," she added, meaning William's younger brothers. "Though it seems there's always trunks to pack and unpack, always someone coming or going."

Elizabeth sorted the clothes Mammy took from the trunks. "This will be the last time we unpack trunks from boarding school, at least for a while. Mr. Will and I have decided the girls will be better educated at home." *Better educated—and at a savings,* she thought. "Miss Rebecca and I will undertake their schooling after the summer holiday." As the oldest of Will's half sisters, Rebecca was more help than burden.

"Miss Bec's looking peaked lately." Mammy closed the trunk lid.

"I've noticed that too. We'll have to keep an eye on her."

When summer was over, Elizabeth and Rebecca set up their little school in a room off the kitchen. It was the first time either of them had taught and they laughed and prayed their way through lesson plans. Then Elizabeth noticed Rebecca getting weaker. She began to run a fever, and Elizabeth feared it was tuberculosis, the "Seton complaint." When, after several months of bed rest, Rebecca did not improve, Elizabeth and Will sent her to one of the older Seton sisters in Delaware, Anna Maria Vining, to regain her health away from the activity of the large household. Elizabeth was left to school the children alone.

One morning as she set out books and tablets and as the young Setons and her own Little Paddlers, now three of them, scrambled to their seats, Anna said, "Ma, I miss Aunt Bec."

"I miss her too, Anna." Elizabeth kissed Anna's curls. "We must keep asking God to heal her so she will come back to us soon."

Our little circle has lost its key, Elizabeth thought about her absent sister-in-law. *Oh, dear Bec. I'm truly lost without my soul's sister. You are my support in every way, my example of goodness and virtue and amiable disposition!*

Elizabeth watched Anna imitating first Charlotte, then Mary, Harriet, and Cecilia. Willy and Dick wrote on their slates, too.

"Girls," Elizabeth said, "work on your marking and figures while I listen one by one to each of you reciting the Ten Commandments and naming the states and the divisions of the globe. Then we will all listen to the little pieces you've memorized."

In the afternoon, Elizabeth taught the girls to sew. They cut out dresses from dimity and nightgowns from flannel, while Elizabeth, by now expecting her fourth child, cut out a maternity suit for herself. As she worked, she thought, *Gone are the days when I can have a seamstress make my clothes. But should I complain? I have my dear William, all my darlings, and a Protector who orders all things aright.*

She checked the girls' work. "Well done. Tomorrow we'll ruffle shirts for the boys. The day after we can begin to sew the dresses. But we need to finish up now. I must visit one of my widows," she said, referring to someone from the Society for the Relief of Poor Widows with Small Children, which Elizabeth had established with Rebecca and some other ladies of Trinity Episcopal Church. "Then soon Mrs. Sadler will arrive," she said, referring to a friend of hers. Mammy came in and began putting things away. "You go visit your widow before Mrs. Sad comes."

Elizabeth thrived on her busy life. Besides caring for the young Setons and her own children, supporting Will, and running the household, she was known for her generosity and for bringing peace into situations that needed compassion and prayer. She was often found at the bedside of the sick or dying, which left little time for the social affairs of former days. But she was content and even wrote to Julia that she was happy to be freed of the duties of what some called "the world." Elizabeth's world was her family, her treasure, and now at last she could devote herself to them.

Because Little Dick, her third child, had been such a difficult birth, Dr. Bayley and William arranged for Elizabeth to rest before her fourth child's delivery. Rebecca had written she was at last well enough to return, so she would care for her younger brothers and sisters. And in May, Dr. Bayley put Anna, William, and Dick in his boat and headed for Staten Island, where the city of New York had built him a health station and a home. That left Elizabeth free to do little but prepare herself for the baby. When she felt rested enough, she joined her father and children.

Catherine, nicknamed Kit, was born June 28, 1800. Eight days later, Elizabeth gave a dinner party to celebrate Kit's birth, as well as the safe Atlantic crossing of a Seton cargo ship.

While the women sat on the lawn admiring little Kit and watching the sunset, the men walked down to the water with after-dinner cigars. Elizabeth was pleased to see Will enjoying his friends. The past two years had been a disaster for the shipping business with pirates and the French seizing ships, as well as shipwrecks claiming cargo. It was no wonder that Will feared losing the family fortune. He had still not wholly recovered from his father's death and now faced the shock of a possible Seton business failure, including a lawsuit and bankruptcy. The full weight fell upon him. And with the Seton interests spread among different ports, he didn't even know exactly how the business stood financially. He knew only that he couldn't pay his business bills and he worried how he would support both his father's family and his own.

Again Elizabeth stayed up till one and two in the morning copying correspondence and learning the whys and wherefores of the business so she could support her Will. Will had put his arm around her thickening waist, gently kissed her forehead, and said, "Eliza, My Old Knot of Oak. What should I do without you?"

Elizabeth chose to look at all the events as guided by a just and merciful Protector. The summer itself was blessed indeed. William came to Staten Island four days a week. Her father left only to check disease aboard vessels entering the United States from foreign countries. And she had leisure to pray, read scripture, write letters, walk, and play with the children.

Mornings when Elizabeth stood on the balcony outside her bedroom breathing in the fresh sea air, she could see ships for fifty miles and hear the cries of captains across the water. One morning she watched her father, gun across his arm, tramp off across the fields to hunt snipes and she said aloud, "Consider the blessings that are at his right hand for them that love him."

One afternoon they all went down to the beach and, while Elizabeth read, her father built sandcastles with the children.

"Father, Will comes tomorrow. I propose you sail us to Sandy Hook for a family picnic."

The children squealed with delight. Dr. Bayley put a stick in the castle. "The captain says, 'All for Sandy Hook say aye.'"

"Aye!"

All summer Elizabeth coaxed William to join them like this and to rest in the sun. Mindful not to show her fear, she worried about his health. He showed signs of strain, even though he had become resigned to bankruptcy, where once he had been frantic about it.

The night before they left for the city Elizabeth walked on the porch, with Kit cuddled into her shoulder, watching the setting sun change the clover fields from blue-green to gold, to pink, then sink like a luminous red ball into the sea. The breeze whipped at her dress as she watched a large cloud, like a bank of pure snow, rise over New York City, retaining its whiteness in its center, but very dark beneath. Now and then, it lit up with lightning while the sky over the house was clear and spangled with bright stars. Then a light wind pushed clouds over the bright moon, the thunder clapped, and the rain beat on the porch roof overhead.

Dear God, she thought, *are not the events of my life like this scene? One moment my life is like the sky with the bright moon and spangled stars, the next it's full of storm clouds and rain.*

Elizabeth kissed her daughter's head. "Your father is truly a man of honor," she whispered. "He's determined to pay his debts. Still, I am afraid that he could go to jail. All we own may be seized as payment. We will be totally poverty stricken."

She looked at the clouds. The storm had vanished and all was bright again. *Dear God, should I worry? It is you who orders every occurrence in its time and place. Help me to turn my soul to you, comforter of the afflicted.*

During the next few months, it became clear that William must declare bankruptcy or risk going to jail. Then a few days before Christmas, a man from court arrived and, with Elizabeth watching, listed each piece of furniture, every book, every piece of china, even the children's clothing. Everything could be used to pay the debt. A few weeks later William handed over the keys to the business. In May the Setons moved from their gracious Stone Street family home to a small one on State Street on the Battery.

CHAPTER SIX
THY WILL BE DONE

Elizabeth was overwhelmed with thanksgiving because Will sat next to her in the pew at Trinity Episcopal Church. Silently she prayed, *Gracious God, you have fulfilled my every desire. Will's heart is nearer to me for being nearer to you. Glory to my God for this unspeakable blessing. Glory to my God for the waters of comfort and conviction which flow through your ministering servant, our blessed Reverend Hobart. Thank you for this pious friend who has soothed and comforted my troubled soul. It is he who brought my Will, my own, back to you.*

Elizabeth and William stood when Reverend John Henry Hobart, a curate of Trinity Episcopal Church, entered the sanctuary. Though the young priest was short and wore thick spectacles, he inflamed hearts with love for God as he conducted the service, read the scriptures out loud and, without notes, preached like a father entreating his children to hear the truth and to choose light instead of darkness.

It was Friend Hobart, as Elizabeth called him, who directed Elizabeth's troubled soul during Will's declining health, the family's financial difficulties, her father's death from yellow fever, and Mammy's death. It was Friend Hobart who helped her come to accept these two deep losses. When they prayed "Thy will be done" in the Our

ELIZABETH ANN SETON

Father, Elizabeth would finger the little gold cross on her watch chain her father had given her and remember how, as he was dying, they too had repeated together, over and over, "Thy will be done." It was also Friend Hobart who baptized Little Bec, her fifth child, and who asked Elizabeth and Rebecca to minister to the poor, sick, and dying. And it was Friend Hobart who at last brought Will back to the church.

Elizabeth remembered the day William decided to give his life to the Lord in earnest. He had walked into the nursery carrying an open Bible in his hands.

"I've been reading the scripture for today: 'What does it profit a man to gain the whole world if he loses his soul?'" Will stood quietly a moment. "It cut me to the quick when our Friend Hobart spoke of the uncertainty of the time of Christ's coming, a personal day of judgment, and how foolish worldly things will seem when we see our Redeemer face to face. I realized I toil and toil and what is it? What I gain destroys me daily soul and body. I'm full of shame and sorrow that I have been as a heathen before God." He closed the Bible. "But that is all behind me now. I can begin to love God as I ought to have done all these years."

Elizabeth remembered kissing William gently. "Oh dearest Will, it's true," she answered. "The Lord remembers not our past but casts our sins away from us, as far as the East is from the West."

After Sunday service, while Kit napped and Elizabeth nursed baby Bec, she thought, *This truly is the Lord's Day to me. Will is reading scripture, all my children are healthy, and I can hear the sounds of Anna, Willy, and Dick hallooing at strollers across the street on their way to the Columbia Gardens for an afternoon concert.*

"Lord," she prayed aloud, "You *are* my Shepherd and I rest within your fold. I give myself and all that I call mine to you—my Will's health, our finances, our children. Only keep me in your grace and I shall strive to serve you always."

Although she prayed fervently for Will's health to improve, he declined rapidly and everyone feared the end was near. Elizabeth was grieved to the depths of her soul. The doctors suggested a sea voyage, so in spite of protests from all sides, William and Elizabeth decided to visit his dear friends, the Filicchis, in Leghorn, Italy. Eight-year-old Anna would go with them, while the other children were left behind with relatives.

Elizabeth wrote her friend, Eliza Sadler, that everyone thought they were mad to make such a journey, especially since Will's health had so drastically worsened. She and Will would grasp at any possibility of recovery, but in the end, God was their only hope. Elizabeth's spirit trembled at what lay ahead of her. She asked Eliza to take her darlings in her arms often during their absence.

Before their journey Elizabeth sold her valuables, saying adieu to each one, happy to be separated from the things of the world. She asked the Hobarts to keep the beloved picture of Christ the Redeemer which she found in her father's belongings, her pianoforte, and her escritoire (little writing desk), until her return. Then, with faith in their Leghorn journey, Elizabeth closed the house.

As the ship passed the Battery, Elizabeth, concealing her tears, waved to the children with her red handkerchief. William wept, too weak to conceal his tears.

Once out to sea, he slept better and coughed less, but ate little and sweat most of the time. Still, Elizabeth delighted in the ocean sunrises and sunsets and the play of the moonlight on the waves. She prayed many *Te Deums* at the ship's rail: *You are God: We praise thee. You are the everlasting Father: All creation worships thee. In you, Lord, do we hope and we shall never hope in vain.* She had leisure to pray, read scripture to William, teach Anna the meaning of the psalms, and write daily in a journal for Rebecca.

When the ship was in the bay of Gibraltar, Elizabeth dreamed she was climbing an immense black mountain. When she was near the top, almost exhausted, a voice said, "Never mind, take courage, there is a beautiful green hill on the other side, and on it an angel waits for you."

After seven weeks at sea, the ship pulled into port to the welcome of Ave Maria bells. The following morning as they excitedly made preparations to go ashore, Elizabeth said, "Listen, Anna, a band is playing 'Hail, Columbia.'" They went on deck and watched an Italian official board and argue with the captain. Then, with the grim-faced Italian standing at attention next to him, the captain announced, "The Italian government has been advised there is yellow fever aboard the ship. I have denied it to no avail. They are demanding that all who are ill be quarantined for a month."

The announcement was a blow. William looked as if he would not live out the day, so of course the quarantine would apply to him. They went below to their cabin and Elizabeth, choking back tears, said to Anna, "Stay with Papa." Hiding herself in her berth so that William and Anna could not see her, she wept bitter tears. Finally, exhausted from crying, Elizabeth helped Will from his berth, took Anna's little hand and, with William leaning heavily on her, returned to the deck.

Fearing yellow fever, no one dared touch them or any of their belongings, except the Italian Capitano assigned to help them and required to stay in quarantine as well. They climbed aboard an open boat with fourteen oarsmen. Lashed by wind and cold spray, they rode for an hour over rough seas until they finally reached a canal with a chain across the entrance. Bells rang, the chain was let down, there was more rowing between high cement walls as they listened to the quarrels of seamen in a foreign language— then finally the boat landed. A guard pointed the way with his bayonet. Bystanders watched Elizabeth, with Anna alongside, struggle to support her tottering William.

Mrs. Filippo Filicchi had come to welcome them; however, she had to stay on the other side of a high fence. Though a native of Boston herself, she spoke to the guard in Italian. He shook his head emphatically and answered in short, gruff sentences.

Sorrowfully she said to the Setons in English, "This is a sad welcome to our country. My husband's dear friend, you look so sick. I have tried to convince the guard that you don't have yellow fever, but he will not listen. We will do all we can to care for you. Meanwhile, my husband will see the authorities."

The guard signaled the Setons to follow him. They climbed twenty stone steps then entered Room No. 6, a high-arch-ceilinged room with a brick floor, whitewashed stone walls, and one barred window. The window's wooden shutters were notched all over with the number of days the occupants had been interred. When the door clanged shut and was bolted from the outside, Elizabeth noticed slips of paper on the door where others had marked the days. She asked herself: *When **our** days are ended, will my dear William be alive?*

Coughing violently, William fell down on the mattress on the floor. Cold emanated from the bricks and walls. The three Setons shivered. Anna clung to Elizabeth and whispered in her ear, "Mama, if Papa should die here...but God will be with us." After a while, Anna found the rope that had tied her box and began jumping to warm herself.

Elizabeth knelt in a recess in the wall, weeping until tears washed the bricks. Feeling abandoned by God, she could not pray. Rising, she looked out the window at the waves beating against the rocks at the entrance to their prison. She felt wind howl through every crevice as it filled the room with smoke from the charcoal fire. Bitterly she thought, *My husband has left all to seek a milder climate and here is confined within these damp walls, exposed to the cold and the winds that penetrate to the very bones; without a fire—except the charcoal which oppresses his breast so as nearly to convulse him. What is to become of us?*

Elizabeth's bitterness shocked her to her senses. *O God, forgive me for shutting you out of my soul,* she prayed. *You are my only friend and resource in my misery. You are the only consolation of my soul. Do not abandon us in our time of trial. Have mercy on us and give us strength.* Then, having regained her peace, she returned to Anna and William with a smile.

In a little while the Capitano brought them three warm eggs, wine, and bread, but William could not eat. He shuddered, then coughed up blood. After Elizabeth tended to him they prayed together, then he fell asleep. Anna, with tears streaming down her face, said her prayers. Elizabeth read her scriptures on trusting in God until she, too, fell asleep.

The days passed slowly and each day mirrored the previous one: Four bells rang on the hour. The Ave Maria bells rang at sunset. Then an hour later the bells for the dead rang to remind Catholics to pray for the souls in purgatory. Elizabeth became reconciled to bolts and bars and to their gray-haired Capitano with his cocked hat and kind face who brought a bouquet for her and a doll for Anna. The Filicchis sent beds and curtains, and brought warm food every day, but they could not obtain a release.

It was Advent, so every day Elizabeth and Anna knelt on mats next to William's bed to read their daily service and sing hymns. He followed, making the prayers his own, kissing the cross, and whispering, "My Jesus, my Redeemer, thy will be done."

Will took Elizabeth's hand and whispered, "My life, my soul, my dearest of women." He closed his eyes a few minutes, and then opened them again. "I miss Hobart's friendship. I sorely missed a man's friendship after Father died. And my darlings so far away." He sighed, "But I shall look forward to us meeting as one family in heaven."

Elizabeth kissed his forehead, "When you awake in that world, you will find that nothing could tempt you to return to this."

He shivered continually, and Elizabeth and Anna rubbed his hands and feet to keep them warm. He groaned and vomited blood. Elizabeth cleaned him with tenderness, thinking, *Lord, I not only wait on William, I wait on you in William.* She prayed, *Heavenly Father, I know these contradictory events are permitted and guided by the light of thy wisdom. Help me to keep in mind your infinite mercy which permits sufferings of the perishable body, so the soul has an opportunity of obtaining eternal life. Then I shall find that "all things have worked together for our good."*

Elizabeth gave Will a few sips of milk and some medication for pain and he slept. While she read the Bible, she felt her guardian angel's presence and looked up from her book. Later she wrote in her journal to Rebecca that if she had forgotten God for a single moment during their quarantine, if she had not been able to find his comfort and consolation in scripture, she would have gone mad.

One Sunday when the bells rang five o'clock, Elizabeth thought, *It is noon at home and all my dear ones will be at the altar receiving the sacrament.* Kneeling in a corner she prayed, *Heavenly Father, if the cup of salvation cannot be received visibly in this strange land, please by the blessing of Christ may I receive it by desire. Oh my soul, what can shut us out from him who dwells in us through love?*

Later one night, Elizabeth knelt by William's bed. Hiding her tears from him, she relived spring at Uncle Bayley's farm—all those sweet hours under the tree where she praised God.

"O God," she whispered, "Wintry storms of time shall pass, and unclouded spring will be enjoyed forever. With you there is no prison with high walls, no bolted doors, no sorrow for the soul that lives in you amidst present trouble and a gloomy future. While I live, in time or in eternity, I will sing praise to you who holds up my soul in hope."

Elizabeth's hope was not unfounded. A few days before Christmas, five days earlier than expected, the Filicchi family sent their carriage and two servants, who carried William out. The fifteen-mile ride to an apartment in Pisa on the Arno River seemed to enliven William, but when he tried to walk alone, he could not, and the servants helped him into bed. He slept most of the time except when the Setons prayed together. At midnight on Christmas Eve, he awoke and said to Elizabeth, "You have not been to bed."

"No, Love, for the sweetest reflections keep me awake; Christmas Day is begun, the day of our Redeemer's birth."

"Yes," he answered. "How I wish we could have the sacrament."

"Well, we must do all we can." Elizabeth poured some wine in a glass, said different parts of the psalms and the prayers of the Episcopalian communion service, and they drank the cup of thanksgiving.

"I thank God that he has given me so much time to pray and reflect," Will said. "Such consolation in his word and in prayer." He handed the cup to Elizabeth. "My Jesus, thy will be done."

Two days later, William charged the captain of the ship with Elizabeth's and Anna's safety to America. The following day, with the name of Jesus on his lips, and with a strong pressure of the hand which he had agreed to give her in the moment that Jesus should come for him, Elizabeth's beloved William died.

CHAPTER SEVEN
Bless Me with Faith

On the day of William's death, Mrs. Amabilia Filicchi took Elizabeth and Anna to Leghorn. Putting her arm around Elizabeth's shoulder, she said, "Come, Elizabeth, I will take you and Annina home now." (*Annina* in Italian meant "little Anna.")

Elizabeth's head jostled against the hard surface of the carriage. She held Anna close thinking, *God, you are my God. I am alone in the world with you and my little ones, but you are my Father and doubly theirs.*

At Leghorn the carriage drew up to a large square house. Antonio Filicchi, a slim, dark-haired, aristocratic-looking man, helped his wife from the carriage, then extended his hand to Elizabeth. "My dear Elizabeth, I am so sorrowful about my worthy friend." Then he lifted Anna down. "Poor child," he said with such a look of sympathetic kindness that Elizabeth had to fight back the tears. "Come, I show you to your rooms."

He led the way through spacious, richly-furnished rooms into a sitting room, adjoined to a large bedroom with a smaller one behind it. "My Amabilia took liberty to find the widow's clothes for you." He gestured toward the bed on which lay a long black dress, a short black cape, and a white cap. "You must consider this your home and we are your family. We serve you now."

That night Elizabeth greeted a dozen people who had come to express their sympathy. The last was the dear old Capitano, with his cocked hat draped in black crepe; his face was so full of sorrow that Elizabeth's heart ached the more.

The next day William was buried. The news of his death and his poor little widow and her young daughter brought every American and British person in Leghorn to the services. After the funeral, Elizabeth wrote to Rebecca, relating William's last hours. She asked her to tell the others, for she had not the strength to write each separately.

That evening after Elizabeth and Anna said their prayers together, Anna burst into tears, "O Mama, I know Papa is praising God in heaven, and I ought not to cry for him, but I believe it is human nature, is it not, Mama?"

"Yes, my darling. It is human nature." Elizabeth held Anna in her arms and they wept together.

In the days that followed, Elizabeth rested then began to participate in the household routine. She was touched by the piety and religious devotion of this Catholic family.

Afternoons, she and Anna accompanied Mr. and Mrs. Filicchi and their young children on their walk. They always stopped at a church to "visit Christ really present in the tabernacle, the little gold house on the back of the altar," Amabilia explained.

Elizabeth slowly knelt in a pew, overwhelmed by the idea that God was really present on the altar. She covered her face with her hands. Tears slipped through her fingers. *Oh, to believe what these dear souls believe,* she thought.

Evenings, after dinner, she listened to their explanations of their faith, but said little.

"We believe Jesus is really present in the bread and wine by the power of the Holy Spirit," Antonio explained. "It is not the priest who transforms it. No, it is the power of God who does so."

"If we live a good life," Amabilia added, "we can receive him every day. He then lives in us and acts through us. It is wonderful, is it not?"

Elizabeth thought, *No wonder they look as happy as angels. How could one have even the smallest trouble in the world!* Episcopalians believed that the Lord's Supper is a symbol and memorial of the body and blood of Christ. She remembered how she and Rebecca, running from one church to another and receiving the sacrament in each, would sigh and say, "No more until next Sacrament Sunday."

One evening Mr. Filicchi suggested, "Elizabeth, it is many weeks before your ship sails. Why not see some of our beautiful Italy? My Amabilia is surely happy to take you and Annina to Florence."

"William loved Florence and was eager for me to see it. Yes, I would like to see scenes that meant so much to him," Elizabeth said thankfully.

In Florence they stayed at the famous Medici Palace overlooking the Arno River with its five bridges, which were always thronged with people and carriages. She visited churches, art galleries, and museums with an aching heart, remembering how William talked about their going together, thinking how he would have pointed out the beauties of every object.

In the Chapel of the Most Holy Annunciation, Elizabeth stopped short at the sight of hundreds of people kneeling in prayer in the candlelit church. She found the first empty pew, bowed her head to hide her weeping, and said her little service until the Mass was over and the organ ceased. At Santa Maria Novella Church she gazed up at a life-sized painting of the descent from the cross, and thought, *Dear Mary, the agony on your face is like the agony in my soul.*

Walking down the steps of the church, Anna whispered, "Ma, are there no Catholic churches in America? Will we not go to the Catholic Church when we get home?"

Elizabeth and Anna spent evenings in their room saying their service, reading the scriptures and *The Imitation of Christ,* and talking about their day. Elizabeth's heart cried out for her other little ones. She fondled Anna's curls, grateful to have her oldest there to be a companion and to soothe her grief.

A few weeks later the maid handed Elizabeth a letter from Antonio. Addressing her as his sister, Antonio wrote that he was praying for her and that he asked God to give her the strength to see that true happiness lay in religion. "Knock at the door," he advised her, "and you will be heard."

Elizabeth thought, *Antonio sees how I am being drawn to his faith. How gently he encourages me.*

When they returned to Leghorn, she learned their ship had been damaged and would take weeks to repair. She could not hide her disappointment. Her arms ached for her little ones. But there was nothing to be done and her life continued as before, now beginning each day with Mass in the Filicchis' private chapel.

One day Elizabeth was visiting the Church of Montenero, a place of pilgrimage. At the very moment of the consecration, a young Englishman whispered loudly in her ear, "This is what they call their 'real Presence.'"

Involuntarily, Elizabeth bent from him to the floor. Tears stung her eyes and St. Paul's words went through her mind,

"Anyone who eats and drinks, without understanding that it is Christ's Body, eats and drinks a sentence of judgment against himself." *Yet,* she wondered, *how could they eat and drink their own damnation for not understanding it, if the Blessed Sacrament is but a piece of bread? And how could his body be there? And how did he breathe my soul into me?* One question tumbled over another in her mind.

After dinner one night, Elizabeth asked, "Dear Mr. Filicchi, if there is but one faith, and nobody pleases God without it, where are all the good people who die out of it?"

He answered gently, "I don't know. That depends on what light of faith they had received; but I know where people will go who can know the right faith if they pray for it and inquire concerning it and yet do neither." At that time, some Catholics believed that only Catholics would go to heaven.

Elizabeth laughed, "Are you saying, sir, that you want me to pray and inquire and be of your faith?"

"Pray and inquire," he answered. "That is all I ask."

Elizabeth thought that surely everyone must be respected in his own manner of seeing things. Yet she decided to pray. So each day she prayed in the words from a poem by Alexander Pope: "If I am right, O teach my heart still in the right to stay. And if I'm wrong, thy grace impart to find the better way."

Mr. Filicchi gave Elizabeth books to help her understand the Roman Catholic Church. She prayed and read, and read and prayed. The discussions after dinner grew longer. She was drawn to the church but had not the faith to embrace the Catholic teaching. In the final days before the ship sailed, she still had only the desire but not the faith.

Finally, the day arrived when Elizabeth and Anna boarded the ship for America. As they said their goodbyes, Elizabeth discovered that Anna had a fever and asked the ship's doctor to examine her. He reported, "The little lass has scarlet fever. You cannot sail on this ship. She will soon be a very sick girl. And the fever is contagious."

The news was a blow! Not only must they delay their return, but scarlet fever easily meant death in the 1800s. Elizabeth feared for Anna's life.

While Elizabeth kept vigil by Anna's bedside for three weeks, the Filicchi household secured their every need. Then scarcely had Anna recovered when Elizabeth herself contracted the disease and was three weeks in bed as well. She and Anna were cared for with such attention that she marveled at the goodness and mercy of these Catholics.

One afternoon while she was recuperating, Elizabeth sat in the chair next to her window reading. She heard little bells ringing in the street below. She thought, *The priest is carrying Jesus, my Redeemer, in the Blessed Sacrament to someone who is sick. Oh God, how happy I would be, even so far away from all so dear, if I could find you as they do.* Without thinking, she fell on her knees. "O God," she cried, "you see that my whole soul desires only you. If you are really there, bless me with faith." Rising, she then picked up a prayer book Mrs. Filicchi had left on the table. Elizabeth opened it at random and read aloud a prayer of St. Bernard to the Blessed Virgin: "Remember, O most gracious Virgin Mary, that never was it known that anyone who implored your help or sought your intercession was left unaided. Inspired by this confidence I fly unto you, O Virgin of Virgins, my Mother. To thee I come, before thee I stand, sinful and sorrowful. O Mother of the Word Incarnate, despise not my petitions, but hear and answer me. Amen."

After saying the prayer, Elizabeth felt she truly had the mother she had missed as a child. She cried herself to sleep on Mary's heart.

The weeks passed with Elizabeth praying for faith and observing the good example of all in the Filicchi household. During the Lenten season, she noticed that Amabilia did not eat until three in the afternoon. One day Elizabeth asked her the reason for her fasting.

Amabilia explained, "I fast for my sins, and for those who do not know God. I unite my weakness from fasting with our Savior's sufferings."

Elizabeth remembered one Ash Wednesday back in New York when, after a good breakfast of buckwheat cakes and coffee, she had prayed: "I turn to you in fasting, weeping, and mourning." Feeling foolish by this paradox, she had asked Reverend Hobart what was meant by fasting in their prayer book. He had answered vaguely that it was an old custom.

One evening Elizabeth asked, "Antonio, I see you make a sign before your prayers. Could you show it to me?"

"We call it the Sign of the Cross. I show you." Antonio stood by the window with the moon shining full on his face. Raising his eyes to heaven, he touched his forehead saying, "In the name of the Father," then touching his heart he said, "and of the Son," and touching each shoulder he said, "and of the Holy Ghost."

Elizabeth reverently followed his example. Chills ran through her body. *The Sign of the Cross of Christ on me!* she thought, recalling the scripture where the angel is to sign each person on the forehead with a cross. *Oh, to be so*

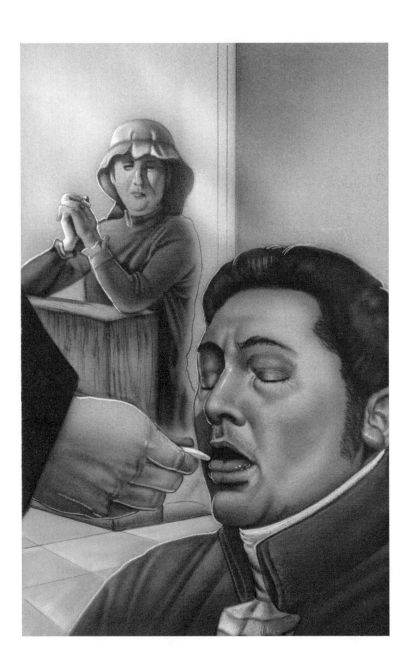

closely united with him who died on it. Oh, that last day, when it is to be borne in triumph.

Antonio explained, "We believe that all we do and suffer can be offered for our sins and serves to make amends for them."

Overwhelmed with love for her dear Savior, Elizabeth wanted to be alone with him. "Please excuse me, Antonio. I will go to my room now."

In April, the ship was ready. Amabilia suggested that, because of hostile cruisers and pirates, it was too dangerous a journey for Elizabeth and Anna to make alone and Antonio should accompany them. He agreed, saying he could also check on his American business interests while there.

The day before they sailed, Antonio took Elizabeth to visit William's grave. Weeping without restraint, she remembered the happiness of former years and her husband's last sufferings.

In the carriage back to the Filicchi house, Elizabeth confided her fears for the future. "Antonio, what will become of us? I have no home, no money. In fact, we are in debt. I cannot work just now. My children are too young and need me."

Antonio answered, "My sister, Almighty God is laughing at you. He takes care of the little birds and makes the lilies of the field to grow, and you fear he will not take care of you? I tell you, he will take care of you."

The next morning the stars were still shining when they entered the chapel for Mass before boarding the ship in two hours. Elizabeth watched Amabilia and Antonio go to communion and she thought, *What a picture of faith and reverence they are. Dear God, I beg you, please give me their faith. I promise I will give you all in return for this most precious gift.*

ELIZABETH ANN SETON

Tearfully Elizabeth and Anna kissed the Filicchi household goodbye. Then Elizabeth watched the tenderness of Antonio's parting from his wife. *Such a union is in God,* she thought. *They shall not be separated although he will be thousands of miles away.*

In the rosy glow of dawn, Amabilia stood on the balcony and waved goodbye. Then at the final signal from the sailing vessel, the carriage bore them away.

CHAPTER EIGHT
ON GOD HIMSELF
I PIN MY FAITH

Elizabeth, her arm around Anna, stood next to Antonio at the ship's rail, watching the large red sun change into a luminous puddle on the horizon, then sink into the sea.

"Six days more until I hold my little ones," Elizabeth said. "Yet I am thankful for this time for you to instruct me and answer my questions. It has helped my understanding of you Catholics. I am convinced now I must join your faith."

"I want you to be certain. It would be wise to talk to your spiritual advisor, Reverend Hobart. It is a—how do you say?—a big step."

"Yes. I fear the effect my change of religion will have on my friendship with dear Hobart," Elizabeth said thoughtfully. "Perhaps I should send a letter to him with the clipper that will come alongside this morning to take the mail."

"Good. You write your letter and Annina and I will find something to amuse ourselves. Won't we, Annina?" Antonio put a fatherly arm around Anna.

Elizabeth went to her cabin and wrote to Reverend Hobart. She asked him to respect her decision to change to the Roman Catholic faith, begged him to remain her brother, and told him his friendship was so dear to her she could not stand being separated. However, if his friendship was the cost she had to pay for becoming Catholic, she would pay it. She knew, from William's death, that through such loss God would only draw her all the closer. When she put down her pen, she thought, *I fear I shall be abandoned by all those close to me if I join the Catholic religion. My God, I cling to you, for who have I in heaven but you and who on earth?*

The ship arrived in New York on June 4, 1804. With a racing heart, Elizabeth looked over the ship's rail. She scanned a sea of faces on the dock. *Little Dick!* Her heart sang out as she caught sight of Cecilia holding her son Richard. And there was her sister Mary holding darling little Bec, while Brother Wright Post held Kit's and William's hands. Now Elizabeth saw Sam Seton and his sisters— Harriet, Charlotte, and Mary. There was William's other brother James and his wife Mary, William's friend John Wilkes, and Elizabeth's godmother Mrs. Sarah Startin. And there was dear Eliza Sadler and her husband.

Holding Anna's hand, Elizabeth ran down the gangplank onto the dock. She scooped her little ones into her arms, laughing and crying at once. "Anna, look how Willy's grown. Dick, you're so tall. Kit, dear sweet Kit!" She hugged little Bec. "Do you remember Mama?" *Oh, dear God,* she thought, *my poor fatherless children. But you are the Father of the fatherless and the Helper of the helpless.*

Elizabeth greeted as many as she could, then introduced them to Mr. Filicchi. It was then she realized someone was missing. "Where is Rebecca?" she asked.

Cecilia looked grave. "Rebecca has the Seton complaint like Brother Will. She's very ill and has been holding on only for you."

Elizabeth held her sister-in-law, unable to answer because of the tightness in her throat.

Following her return, Elizabeth lived with Mary and Wright Post but visited Rebecca every day, often staying the night, struggling to resign herself to this additional loss. She told Rebecca all she had learned about the Roman Catholic religion, and Rebecca responded with faith in the words of Ruth from the Old Testament: "Your people will be my people and your God, my God." Then on a Sunday morning in July, Rebecca died.

At the cemetery Elizabeth thought that all the plenty of her past was gone now forever. She had lost her husband, her soul's sister, her home, and her comfort and in exchange received only poverty and sorrow. Then she stopped her despondent thoughts and willed herself to conquer this new adversity with God's help. *Poverty and sorrow, well, with God's blessing, you too shall be changed into dearest friends,* she thought. *Through you, my soul will discover the palm of victory, the triumph of faith, and the sweet footsteps of my Redeemer leading directly to his kingdom. Then let me gently meet you, welcome you, and be daily carried.*

Soon afterwards Elizabeth wrote to her dear friend Julia, thanking her for her letter of sympathy after Rebecca's death. She also told Julia that dear Will died thinking all was well financially, but that they were in great debt and wholly dependent on the goodness of others. John Wilkes, Wright Post, and Mrs. Startin had all contributed to their maintenance this year, but when little Bec was older, Elizabeth intended to find another means of support. For now, she had a small house a half mile from town, where they occupied the upper room and rented out the lower floor. Elizabeth considered her poverty an opportunity to bring

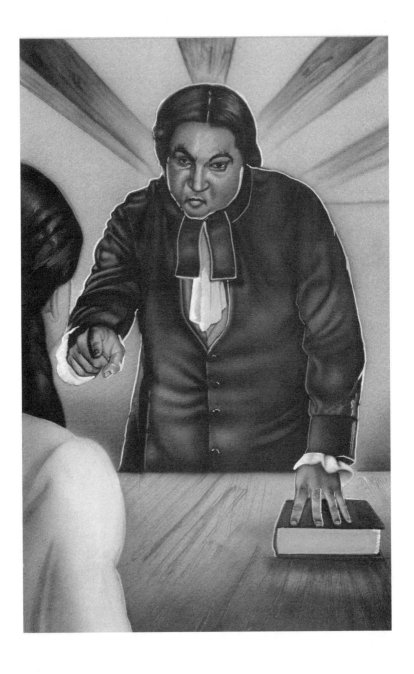

up her children without the dangers of spoiling them. She closed her letter with the comment that, since Rebecca's death, a cave was better suited to her mood than society, but that God had given her many duties. She would try to fulfill his will and not her own.

Julia sent $300 by the next post. Elizabeth was overwhelmed by her faithful friend's generosity. Other friends gave money as well but told her exactly how to spend it, making Elizabeth feel like a child who could not be trusted. However, she thought this would purify her rebellious nature, which could only be a help while she was seeking God's will in her decision to embrace the Catholic faith.

Soon all New York buzzed with the news that Elizabeth Seton was considering joining the Roman Church. She had not heard from Reverend Hobart since her return and wondered how her letter had affected their friendship. Then one day she was surprised by a visit from him.

"How good to see you," she said, offering him her hand. "Come in. Will missed you so and talked about you in his last days. Please sit down."

"Thank you, Elizabeth." Reverend Hobart was stiff, the old friendliness gone. "I received your letter and I shall come right to the point. When I see you, whose sincere and ardent piety I have always thought worthy of imitation, in danger of joining a church which in my judgment is corrupt and sinful, I'm deeply affected by it." He thumped a book he was holding with his fist. "My soul is most anxious and asks, How will you answer to your Almighty Judge for such a decision?"

As he continued to argue most convincingly against the Roman faith, Elizabeth's new Catholic principles were shaken.

"I've brought you a book," he said, handing it to her and rising. "It should help you know the truth about these Catholics."

That night Elizabeth went to bed but lay awake with Reverend Hobart's questions echoing in her ears. "How can you believe that there are as many gods as there are millions of altars and tens of millions of sacred hosts all over the world?"

She thought, *It is God who does it, the same God who fed so many thousands with the little barley loaves and fishes, multiplying them in the hands that distributed them.* "Nothing in it is so very hard to believe, since it is you who does it," she said aloud to the Lord. Then she remembered reading that when we say a thing is a miracle and we do not understand it, we say nothing against the mystery itself; we merely confess our limited knowledge and understanding which does not understand a thousand other things that we must say are true. She reasoned that if the Catholic religion, which gave the world the comforting belief of the presence of God in the Blessed Sacrament, were simply the invention of priests and men, as Protestants said, then God seemed not to desire our happiness as much as the inventors desired it.

Still arguing against Hobart's questions at dawn, she begged once more for faith: *Faith is a gift to be diligently sought and earnestly desired, and I shall groan to you for it and trust one day this storm will cease.*

Reverend Hobart sent other books and documents. They so contradicted what Elizabeth had witnessed in Italy and learned from Antonio that she became confused and troubled. The more she tried to sort out the truth, the more entangled her thoughts became. Week after week she read and prayed. She could not eat or sleep. Her health declined.

She fasted and cried out to know the truth without doubts and hesitations. The weeks stretched into months. She begged that the darkness be made light and her confusion be lifted so she would know what to do.

Not only did a storm rage in Elizabeth's soul, it raged outside as well. Blizzards piled snow so high that no one could come or go out of the house. She missed her sister Mary and sisters-in-law Cecilia and Harriet, who had been her only visitors. They would have helped her laugh about not having money for servants to keep the fire going, prepare meals, dress the children, wash dishes, and care for the house. Now she must keep up her own spirits and do the work as well.

One day Antonio visited her. "My little friend," he said, alarmed, "you do not look well. You are too thin. And you look very tired." He pulled a letter from his breast pocket. "Perhaps this will help. I have written to Bishop John Carroll of Baltimore about you and just today received his reply. He gives very wise direction for you."

"O Antonio, thank you. All day and all night I weigh one side and then the other. I can't see any light." Elizabeth held onto the letter like a lifeline. As soon as Antonio left, she read Bishop Carroll's letter. The bishop wrote that, after suffering the trials of interior darkness and doubt, she would certainly receive merciful relief, light, and consolation. Also, he advised Antonio that Elizabeth had read enough to understand the truth. What she needed now was to pray for the grace and strength to answer God's call.

Clasping the letter, she thought of how kind it was that the only bishop in the United States should bother with one poor widow. Then she looked up to heaven and prayed, *You are light, enlighten me to know the truth.*

No doubt remembering Italy, that night Anna coaxed, "Oh Ma, do teach us the Hail Mary."

"Well, if anyone is in heaven, surely our Savior's mother must be there, so why should we not say it?" Elizabeth reasoned aloud.

They all repeated the prayer after her. Even little Bec lisped the words in her baby talk. Elizabeth blessed each child with the sign of the cross she had so recently learned. Then, after tucking the children in bed, she set her candle on a table by the fire and read from *The Imitation of Christ* and from St. Francis de Sales. Would she ever know better how to please God than these Catholics do?

On Sacrament Sunday, Elizabeth went to St. Paul's Episcopal Church. No one returned her greetings. She slid into a pew next to a long-time parishioner and smiled at her, but the woman looked away. At communion when the celebrant said, "The Body and Blood of Christ," she trembled. Afterwards, trying to calm herself, she took out her Catholic prayer book and read, "O Good Jesus, how happy I am to have thee with me. How can I ever thank thee for coming to me." She choked back a sob. *Oh my Savior and My God!* she prayed. *I long for you alone!*

She left the service quickly. *Lord God,* she decided, *I pin my faith boldly on you. I will go peacefully and firmly to the Catholic Church. For if faith is so important to our salvation, I will seek it where true faith first began and seek it among those who received it from God himself. The controversies on it I am quite incapable of deciding. To the Catholics I will go and try to be a good one. May you accept my intention and pity me.*

On Ash Wednesday, February 27, 1805, Elizabeth walked to St. Peter's Catholic Church for Mass. Rounding the corner, her heart leapt at the sight of the cross shining on the top of the steeple, instead of the weathercock of the Episcopal Church. *Here I go, my God. My heart is all yours.*

She entered the small, dark, quiet church, chose a pew and knelt down. As she pondered the little tabernacle and the painting of the crucifixion above it, her heart knew deep, deep peace.

After Mass she spoke to Father Matthew O'Brien. "Father, I am Mrs. Seton. I am an Episcopalian but I would like to join the Catholic Church."

"Ah, yes," said Father O'Brien. "I have heard of you. You must be the little widow with wee ones all New York is up in arms about," he said in a thick Irish brogue. "'Tis good to finally meet you. Let us talk about this decision a bit."

On March 14, after Father O'Brien was assured that Elizabeth understood what she was undertaking as a member of the Catholic Church, he received her profession of faith in all the Roman Catholic Church believes and teaches. Afterward she knelt in front of the altar and said, "Now my heart is locked up with you in your little tabernacle where I shall now rest forever."

A few days later Elizabeth made her first confession, seeing the Lord himself in the compassionate yet firm Father O'Brien. She felt as if the words of absolution unchained her after thirty years of bondage, much like the chains of imprisoned St. Peter fell away at the touch of the divine messenger.

The days of preparation for her first communion sped by. The night before, Elizabeth knelt in prayer, fearing she had not done all she could to make herself worthy. Then, on the morning of Annunciation Day, she dressed and left the house to go to church. Her heart beat with anticipation on the long walk to town, nearer that street, nearer that cross, nearer that tabernacle. At last Christ entered the poor, poor dwelling of her heart, so all his own.

Afterwards, kneeling in the pew, Elizabeth bowed her head. *At last, God is mine and I am his. Let God arise, let his enemies be scattered. You have come, dearest King, to take up your throne. Come take possession of this poor little kingdom.*

She closed her eyes. *My God is here! He sees me! Every desire is before him!* She said the litany of Jesus and the hymn to the Blessed Sacrament, ending with the words: *Faith for all defects supplies, and sense is lost in mystery. My Lord and my God!*

CHAPTER NINE
I AM A CATHOLIC

One Sunday Elizabeth walked into a mob of finely dressed Protestant men milling around St. Peter's Church door, hecklers often present before the Sunday Masses. One of the men sneered in her face, "It's the poor deluded Mrs. Seton. This is no place for a lady. Go back to the Episcopal Church where the gentle folk go. You don't belong here."

"This is the wrong place to be today, Missus," another tormented her. "We're going to tear that cross right off the steeple."

"And set the church afire," another threatened.

Trembling but unshaken, Elizabeth joined the Irish, French, and German immigrants jostling and crowding into the small church. They were poorly dressed, and Elizabeth knew many could neither speak nor write English. How would they ever better themselves politically and socially when the Religious Liberties Act deliberately excluded immigrants? New York was so fiercely anti-Catholic. Her thoughts flew to her successful, educated, well-dressed aristocratic friends and family at Trinity Episcopal Church. Yes, it was a contrast!

All during Mass the mob yelled, "We're going to burn this unholy place to the ground!" A stone smashed through a window, showering Father O'Brien with glass and landing at the foot of the altar. Several men rushed forward and helped the priest brush the glass from his shoulders and hair and clear it away from the altar. As they returned to their seats, Father said, "Let us thank God no one was hurt, and pray for peace and an end to this prejudice against us." Elizabeth knew that an earlier riot outside the church one Christmas had left several people injured.

Distracted from the Mass, she remembered her first conversation with Wright and Mary Post after she had joined the Catholics.

Wright had asked, "Sister Seton, I understand that you go to the Catholic Church. What is the difference?"

"It is the first church, my brother," she answered. "The church that the apostles began."

"But is not every church from the apostles?" he asked.

Her sister interrupted. "Well, apostles or no apostles, let me be anything in the world but a Roman Catholic. A Methodist, Quaker, anything! A Quaker at least is nice and orderly and their dress so becoming. But Catholics!" Mary exclaimed. "Dirty, filthy, ragged, and red-faced. Their church is a horrid place of spitting and pushing."

Elizabeth had swallowed words of defense, following her spiritual director's advice to give only short answers of information in order to avoid an argument.

Later that day Eliza Sadler had visited her, reporting, "Reverend Hobart is warning all of your friends not to listen to your false and dangerous principles."

Elizabeth's thoughts skipped from the prejudice and hostility of family and friends to her financial difficulties and her search for work. Antonio Filicchi had suggested she go to Montreal, Canada, where she could enroll her sons in the Catholic boys' school and teach. Mrs. Startin suggested opening a teashop, John Wilkes a boarding house for boys, and her sister, Mary, a school for small children. *Children too young to be taught the Hail Mary, no doubt,* Elizabeth remembered thinking.

The only serious offer came from a Protestant couple who were opening a girls' boarding school. She could live with them, receive room and board, and educate her children as well. But when Reverend Hobart heard about the school, he spread the news that she and two other Catholics were opening a school to teach the Catholic faith. Eliza Sadler explained to him that the couple was Protestant and that Elizabeth was only trying to support her family. Reverend Hobart tried to undo the damage, but it was too late. The school closed. Having already given up her small house outside of town, Elizabeth had to hurriedly move in with the Posts.

The Posts' house was too far from St. Peter's for Elizabeth to walk, so Dr. Post had driven her there today, as he did every Sunday. As she waited for him after Mass, she was glad the hecklers had left, made to disperse by the police.

"Mrs. Seton, now isn't it good to see you today?" asked Father O'Brien, his blue Irish eyes twinkling. "And how are you getting on with the Posts?"

Elizabeth answered honestly: "There is quite a tension between Mary and me. Finding fish for the Friday abstinence is a difficulty and expense for her. And it is so crowded with us Setons, I look to heaven and beg for grace for all of us."

"We will relieve you of the abstinence then. We Catholics should be charitable to our Protestant friends." Father's eyes grew serious. "And what about the children?"

"I'm afraid, Father, that they hear friends and family mock and ridicule the church, its teaching, and you good priests. Their minds are being poisoned with bad principles of every kind. It's all I can do to keep my saucy boys from mastering me."

Father tipped back and forth from his toes to his heels. "Well now, it would be best for the boys to be away from this nasty gossip. Perhaps your good friend, Mr. Filicchi, may have a solution."

Praying God would pity a poor widow, Elizabeth wrote to Antonio begging for help. They decided a boarding school away from New York's Protestant environment was the answer and began to investigate the possibilities—the Montreal boarding school, St. Mary's in Baltimore, and Georgetown in Washington, D.C.

One afternoon Antonio visited Elizabeth with good news. Georgetown had taken to heart her situation and reduced the tuition for her boys, which Antonio and Bishop Carroll would then pay for her. With renewed hope in God's care, Elizabeth sent the boys off to Georgetown and once again searched for a means of support. Her friend John Wilkes told her about a position at St. Mark's school, overseeing its boarding house for boys. However, he didn't know if the schoolmaster would consider a Catholic or if the parents would put their children in her care.

Wilkes spoke to the schoolmaster himself on her behalf, and Elizabeth was hired. She moved her three youngest out of the Posts into her own home on the Bowery near St. Mark's Church, two miles from the city. When she was settled, she wrote to Julia how cooking, washing, and mending for the twelve students kept her so busy from dawn till night, that she would fall asleep at her prayers. But she earned three dollars a week for each of them!

On Sundays Elizabeth walked to early Mass, ate break-fast and dinner with Catholic friends, received spiritual direction, went to confession, and walked home. She at last had some measure of peace from the gossip of the city, but Eliza Sadler reported to her, "There are a few who say that so much trouble has turned your brain."

"They simply are mistaken, Sad," Elizabeth answered and, after Eliza left, she kissed her crucifix.

One Sunday in 1806, before dinner at a friend's home, Elizabeth met Bishop Carroll for the first time. She entered the parlor and was met by the kindest face she had ever seen.

"Finally we meet, my long distance friend," Bishop Carroll said.

"With much joy and some trepidation on my part," Elizabeth confessed.

The bishop laughed. "I have a good report on your William and Richard."

While Elizabeth listened to the boys' spiritual and intellectual progress, she thought, *No wonder he is father to all the Catholics in America. He has a father's heart!*

Finally, the bishop asked, "Elizabeth, how would you like to be confirmed on Pentecost?"

Under his spiritual direction, Elizabeth grew in her understanding of the Catholic faith. On Pentecost she took the name of Mary, because it reminded her of the mystery of salvation. A few days later, Father Tisserant, a friend, wrote to her that she was suffering martyrdom through the prejudice she endured but that in confirmation she had received the grace to persevere and to bring others to Christ through her example.

Elizabeth soon discovered she needed the fortification of confirmation. Both Cecilia and Harriet, who had lived so long with her after Father Seton's death and who were drawn to the Catholic faith by her example and conversion, were forbidden by the Setons to see her. They were reduced to corresponding through notes delivered by young Sam. Then a few months later, Cecilia, with her clothes tied in a bundle, appeared on Elizabeth's doorstep.

"Oh, Sis, please let me stay with you. You cannot know what I've been through these last few days at my brother's home."

Elizabeth was shocked by Cecilia's grim face and ushered her inside.

"Sis, James and Mary found the books on the Catholic Church I'd bought and hid in my bureau. They thought you gave them to me. They said if you had not changed your religion that I would not think of changing mine. They were so hateful, they threatened to put me on a ship to the West Indies if I continued to pursue the Catholic religion. They also said they would ask Sister Charlotte's husband, Governor Ogden, to petition the legislature to banish you from the state. They said you would be destroyed socially and your children would be begging their bread. Then they sent me to my room to think it over."

Cecilia began to cry, "I obeyed and heard the door lock behind me. I've been locked in my room for four days. This morning they unlocked the door and I left the house." She lifted her tear-stained face. "I left a note saying I loved them and wanted to return to the family, but I believed it was God's will for me to join the Catholic faith."

"Oh poor, dear Cecilia." Elizabeth hugged her. "Of course you can live here. What a nasty time you've had." Elizabeth stroked her hair. "Let's pray the family will change their minds. We'll pray the litany of the Blessed Virgin. How sweet it will be to ask her who bore him to plead our case."

After Cecilia joined the Catholic Church, her sisters Charlotte Ogden and Mary Hoffman Seton wrote to Elizabeth, saying they would never speak to her again, nor was she welcome in their homes. Other family members and former friends also renewed their persecution against her. Someone threatened to burn down her house. Wright Post, her brother-in-law, and Mrs. Startin, her wealthy godmother, withdrew their financial support. Mrs. Startin also had her removed from her will, leaving no hope of inheritance.

Elizabeth was nearly destitute. She worried, if anything happened to her, how she could leave her children in the care of Protestant relatives. Only Harriet remained loyal and wanted to follow Cecilia into the Catholic Church.

Elizabeth became the laughing stock of New York dinner tables. The boys in her charge, influenced by their parents' attitude, lost their respect for her, were surly and unkind, and insulted to her daughters. Finally several of the boys were withdrawn from the school, reducing her income even further.

With the support of Antonio and Bishop Carroll, Elizabeth was able to face this new harassment. Her dear Bishop Carroll encouraged her in letters and, although having returned to Europe, Antonio gave her unlimited access to his United States bank account.

Even so, Elizabeth once more considered leaving the menacing Protestant climate of New York for Montreal. She wrote or spoke to everyone she thought might offer her wise advice. One morning she decided to talk to Father O'Brien after Mass at St. Peter's Church. But Mass was

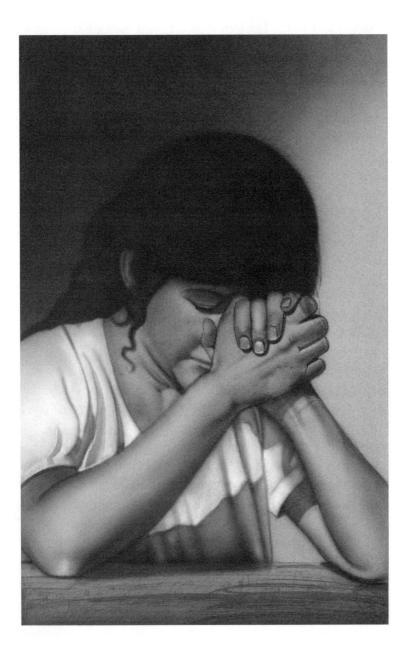

said instead by a visiting priest, Father William Dubourg. Father Dubourg was a founder and president of St. Mary's College in Baltimore. Pouring her heart out to him, she said, "I would like to board at and teach in a convent I know of in Canada where we can be away from this hostile environment. I can keep my children near me and teach in the school there. I had considered this a few years ago and there may be room for us now."

Reverend Dubourg said decidedly, "Come to us, Mrs. Seton. We will help you in your desire for a devout life and the support of your children. We will also assist you in developing a plan of life. We wish to form a small school for the promotion of religious instruction, where you may teach."

"But sir, I have not the talent for it!" Elizabeth replied, astonished.

"We want good example more than talent, Mrs. Seton. I am sure the Lord wants you to further the cause of the Catholic religion in the United States. Of course, I must get approval first, but I believe I can offer you a plot of ground in Baltimore where we could build a house and open a girls' school. It is close to St. Mary's, where your boys could board and go to school. Think it over."

Elizabeth prayed that God would make his will known. She wrote to Antonio, Bishop Carroll, and her priest advisors asking for their wisdom. One of them wrote back: "You are destined, I think, for some great good in the United States." To her amazement, everyone backed the venture, including Wright Post and John Wilkes. So, with thanksgiving for God's mercy, Elizabeth made plans to leave New York for Baltimore.

Before her plans were finalized, a relative of William's, who had been failing rapidly, asked Elizabeth to care for her in her last days. Elizabeth nursed her at night and Cecilia during the day. One morning as Elizabeth was leaving, she overheard Mary Hoffman Seton and Charlotte Ogden in the next room. But instead of the harsh words she expected, Elizabeth heard praise about her and Cecilia's sweetness toward them, as well as their tenderness toward the invalid

"Surely Elizabeth must be weary," Charlotte added, "caring for her children during the day and sitting up all night. Yet she never wavers in her loving care."

At that moment, Cecilia walked through the front door. "Good morning, Sis, how is our dear patient?"

"She's peaceful but the end is near. Very much like when I nursed Mrs. Bayley before her death last year. What a bittersweet memory!" Elizabeth said, thinking of the woman who had forced her from her own home. "I'm still blessed that she called for me in her last days and that we could be reconciled at last." She helped Cecilia off with her coat.

Mary and Charlotte came into the hall. Without her former iciness, Mary said, "Cecilia, the children miss you. Will you not come and visit us soon?"

"And Elizabeth," Charlotte smiled. "Our children ask after you as well. Perhaps you could come to dinner one day," she said in her old friendly manner.

"We would be most happy to. We miss them and you as well," answered Elizabeth, happily surprised by this sudden reversal.

A few days later Will's brother, James Seton, walked into Elizabeth's house, took her in his arms like one of his children and said, as if there had never been trouble between them, "There is a bundle at the Customs House from Italy addressed to E. Seton. Could it be yours? I paid the duty on it and asked the boy to bring it around later."

Watching him mount his horse to leave, Elizabeth wondered about these sudden reconciliations but decided, *So all the world should do!*

In time, James Seton invited Cecilia back to live with his family and to help his wife care for their five children. When his wife Mary died unexpectedly, he asked Cecilia to stay on. Now that there was peace in the family relationships, Elizabeth could look forward to what awaited her in Baltimore.

CHAPTER TEN

THE SWEETEST DREAM
OF MY IMAGINATION

On June 9, 1808, Elizabeth and her three daughters boarded the *Grand Sachem* for Baltimore. Elizabeth sat on the deck with Bec asleep on her lap, watching a young man entertain the other children with a sleight-of-hand trick. Thinking of Cecilia's recent poor health, she hoped that James Seton would soon find someone else to care for his children so that Cis could join them in Baltimore.

After the weeklong voyage, Elizabeth and her daughters ran through the rain to a waiting carriage, which took them to a Mass Bishop Carroll was celebrating to consecrate the new chapel of the Sulpician Priests who founded St. Mary's. As they walked inside, the organ's peal and a burst of song from the choir welcomed them. Anna looked at her mother with surprised delight and whispered, "Ma, so many Catholics! Like us."

After the reception, Father Dubourg took her down a short path behind the chapel and through an opening in a small white fence to the yard of her new house. Looking like a miniature French mansion, it was set like a jewel between two orchards which adjoined St. Mary's seminary where her boys would go to boarding school.

Father Dubourg's sister helped Elizabeth settle in, then two days later she traveled to Georgetown to bring William and Richard, now twelve and ten, home for the summer. In the carriage with her was a priest friend, Michael Hurley, and his recent wealthy convert, Samuel Cooper, who planned to enter St. Mary's Seminary.

Elizabeth loved her new, happier life, once more regulated by the Angelus bells. She attended daily Mass, received communion every day, went to evening benediction, and prayed in the chapel whenever she pleased. The chapel was so close to the house she could hear the bells of consecration and bowed her head at the nearness of her adored Savior. She opened her heart easily to her spiritual director, Father Pierre Babade, who helped her make quick progress in the spiritual life and in understanding the Catholic faith. Her social life could have been active, as she was blessed by many invitations to dine and go on outings to become acquainted with the area, but she usually declined.

Fall came too quickly for the Setons. When the boys went to St. Mary's, Elizabeth took in ten girl boarders, and more from town joined them for religious instruction. Her day began at five-fifteen. By six she was in the chapel, then in her school on Paca Street from nine to three. After school she said the Litany to Jesus with the schoolgirls, then popped back into the chapel before she met with a master of arithmetic who stuffed her brains with dollars and cents, fractions and figures, so that she in turn could teach. At six thirty, she was back in the chapel to say a rosary, make her examination of conscience, and pray Vespers.

One evening after Vespers Father Babade said, with his usual French passion, "I rejoice at the Lord's work in your soul and I believe that the psalm speaks of you when it says, 'The barren woman shall be the joyful mother of children.'"

Puzzled, Elizabeth listened quietly.

"Many of our priests believe, as do I, that you are the one to begin the first establishment of Catholic sisters in the United States. There are two young women from Philadelphia who had planned to enter a convent in Spain, but we would like you to consider an order here."

"Father, I have longed to live a religious life—but to *begin* a new community? I don't have the resources!" she said, stunned. "I am a mother. Whatever Providence has in store for me must be consistent with that. My first duty must always be to my children."

"We feel you do have the talents," he said, patting her hand. "We can make provision for your children when we draw up the rule. However, before we can do anything, we must pray for the financial resources."

"This holy faith I so long resisted is so sweet, so dear to me, that I do wish to do something to promote it, no matter how small," she said thoughtfully. "I'll pray and let the Adored's vote decide."

After Mass one morning, Elizabeth said to Father Dubourg, "Father, after communion I was abandoning my will to the Lord's when I heard our Savior command in a clear voice that I should undertake this, and that Mr. Samuel Cooper would provide the funds."

"I'm delighted with your decision," Father Dubourg said. "But as for Mr. Cooper giving us the money..." he hesitated. "Of course, it is possible. Yet, it might be only your imagination. Let us pray that, if it is God who has spoken to you, he will make his will known also to Mr. Cooper."

"Thank you, Father," she said, at once peaceful.

That very evening after spiritual direction Mr. Cooper asked Father Dubourg why there was no religious community for women in the United States. When Father Dubourg answered that he had desired to begin one for at least fifteen years but lacked the funds, Mr. Cooper offered $10,000 for the project.

"Have you seen Mrs. Seton today?" Father Dubourg asked thoughtfully.

"No," Mr. Cooper replied.

"Have you ever spoken to her about such a project?"

"Never. Are you thinking of trusting her with this affair?"

"Yes. She is here for that purpose. And just this morning she told me she was praying after communion and heard the Lord say that she should ask *you* for the funds. I told her it could be her imagination and she should wait to see if you made an offer."

"God be blessed!" exclaimed Mr. Cooper. "I've been coming to you for a year and we have never before talked about it."

Father Dubourg was still cautious. "I believe that you should pray about this for a month. If you still believe it is God's will, we will be happy to receive your contribution."

A month later Mr. Cooper came with the money. "Sir," he said, "I believe the establishment should be at Emmitsburg, Maryland."

"Surely, you can't mean Emmitsburg!" Father Dubourg was surprised.

"I do not mean to influence the choice of location or the direction the work should take," Mr. Cooper said humbly, "but it will be Emmitsburg. I believe from there it will extend throughout the United States."

ELIZABETH ANN SETON

For several months Elizabeth learned about the religious life from Bishop Carroll, Father Dubourg, and the other Sulpicians. Then, on a blustery, rainy day in March, 1809, she knelt before Bishop Carroll in the lower chapel at St. Mary's and pronounced year-long vows of chastity and obedience, which she could renew or renounce after the year's end. Finishing her vows, Elizabeth began to cry at the enormity of what she was undertaking. *My gracious God! You know my unfitness for this task. I, who by my sins have so often crucified you, I blush with shame and confusion.* She looked up at Bishop Carroll and asked, "How can I teach others, who know so little myself, and am so miserable and imperfect?"

Bishop Carroll, his voice hoarse with emotion at the sight of this humble soul, said, "You shall do it by God's grace, dear lady."

Some time later, Elizabeth wrote Julia about her plans. Mr. Cooper and the Sulpicians had purchased a farm forty miles away at Emmitsburg in the Blue Ridge mountains where Elizabeth would see little of the world. A priest at another seminary and college two miles from their farm would say Mass for them every day, and Father Dubourg would be their superior. He would also regulate their religious exercises and accept or dismiss persons. Their habit would be the Italian widow's dress Elizabeth had worn since William's death.

The sisterhood would be patterned after the Daughters of Charity of St. Vincent de Paul in France. Elizabeth would be head of the community, like the mother of a family, and indeed they already addressed her as "Mother." The community intended to open a free school, with the other sisters teaching the girls and Elizabeth superintending. By this time she had in her little community Cecilia O'Conway from Philadelphia, Anna Maria Murphy from Philadelphia, and Susan Clossey from New York. They still awaited Mary Ann Butler; Rose Landry White, a widow; and Catherine Mullen. Eleanor and Sally Thompson, two sisters from Emmitsburg, also wished to join. Elizabeth's own dear Anna was eager to go to the mountains with them. And Cecilia and Harriet Seton were expected sometime in June. When she arrived Cis was very sick with the Seton complaint, and everyone believed that the mountain air would be good for her.

"I hope when you consider my temper, habits, and disposition," Elizabeth concluded her letter to Julia, "that you will not absolutely disapprove of my resolution, for this is the sweetest dream of my imagination."

On June 21, 1809, Mother Seton, after heartfelt goodbyes, climbed aboard a Conestoga wagon. Inside lay Cecilia, with Harriet close by to care for her. Anna and Anna Maria Murphy sat on either side of Mother Seton, who took the reins. With her spirit soaring, she prayed so all could hear, "The blessed will of him who rules both life and death be done! What is the universe to us—Jesus, our all, is ours, and we are his!"

CHAPTER ELEVEN
A GRAIN OF SEED
FOR ETERNAL LIFE

The farther from Baltimore Mother Seton and her little band traveled, the rougher the road became. They were jarred from side to side in the wagon until Mother at last said cheerfully, "We're being churned like butter. Let's walk until the road gets better."

On the second day they walked four and a half miles before breakfast, except for Cecilia, who lay in the back of the Conestoga. When Elizabeth peeked in to check on her, Cecilia asked, "Sis, what are you all laughing about as you walk?"

Mother Seton smiled. "Never has this country seen the likes of us in our black habits. Everyone comes out to stare, even the dogs and pigs. Some geese from a nearby farm came up to us, stretched their necks, and honked as if to ask, 'Are you any of our sort?' And I answered, 'Yes!'"

By the fourth day, the group was tired but in high spirits, because they knew they would reach Mount St. Mary's, the rustic school and seminary near Emmitsburg, before day's end. The hills grew into foothills and soon Mother could see mountains in the distance and, farther on, St. Mary's Mountain black against the blue sky. She remembered her dream at Gibraltar: "an angel waits for you on the other side." Mother loved the meadows filled with blue cornflowers, Queen Anne's lace, and the fragrance of pink clover. Cattle and horses, sheep and lambs grazed the fields. Her soul filled to overflowing and she exclaimed aloud, "All glory, honor, praise, and thanksgiving to our own loving Father, our faithful friend who will never leave us or forsake us."

Passing through the little village of Emmitsburg, they made their way halfway up the mountain to Mount St. Mary's where they were met by Father John Dubois, the local priest, because Father Dubourg had been detained.

After the women rested, Father Dubois broke the news that their stone farmhouse was not ready, but they could stay in his own house, while he moved into another dwelling on the mountain. They gathered what belongings they could carry and, with Mother Seton cheering them on, climbed a yet steeper path. Awed by the meadows and fields far below like a patchwork quilt in shades of green, she said, "Father, this is incredible! We are halfway in the sky."

In a few days, Mother Seton truly began to feel like a mother. She gently directed the daily prayer and work and helped Harriet in her resolution to join the church.

At the end of July the last wagon arrived with the other sisters, her sons, and two pupils from the Paca Street School in Baltimore. A few days later, Father Dubourg arrived and took them down to the farmhouse in the valley. He apologized for it being too small for sixteen of them. "But," he quickly added, "we will start to build you a new larger house that will be finished by Christmas. And I will send a request by Father Flaget to the good sisters in France for their rule of life. He will be sailing there next month. It is very slow having to send letters across the ocean."

Mother looked around at the primitive conditions, knowing many of the women like herself came from wealthy families. There was one fireplace for the two lower and two upstairs rooms, no running water, and no beds. They would have to sleep with their mattresses on the floor. It would surely be cramped, yet six more waited to join them.

Father eagerly showed her a little alcove off one of the first floor rooms where, after his visit to Baltimore, he planned to build an altar for the Blessed Sacrament and close it with a door they could open for Mass and devotions.

On their first Sunday, the women walked to the village parish for Mass. Other times, with no road or bridge over the creek, they climbed fences, lost their way in the woods en route to the Church on the Mountain, lifted their skirts to jump from stone to stone with shouts of laughter, teetering to keep their balance. Mother rejoiced in their delight at simple pleasures. After Mass they stopped to have a picnic breakfast at a grotto where huge rocks, covered with green moss, hung over a clear stream flowing down from the hill. Someone had placed a cross and a picture of the Blessed Mother nearby.

Moved by the beauty of the little grotto, Mother said, "Before we eat our ham and cream pies, let us sing the Canticle of the Three Young Men in the Fiery Furnace from the Book of Daniel." They all found places to sit down and Mother sang, "Blessed are you, O Lord, God of our Fathers."

"Praise and exalt him, now and forever," the sisters sang in answer.

When they returned to the Stone House, Mother directed them to sit under the trees while she announced the results of the election of the first officers of their little community.

Watching their faces, she said, "Sister Rose will be my assistant, and Sister Cecilia will be secretary and have charge of the school. Sister Kitty will be in charge of housekeeping. Sister Sally will manage the household monies and make purchases." Mother was pleased that they all looked content with her choices. "We will live by temporary rules until the rule of Saint Vincent can be delivered to us from France. Still we will have order to our life." She consulted a slip of paper on which she and Father Dubourg had drawn up a schedule. "We will rise at five, say morning prayers together, make a private meditation, then walk over the mountain to Mass. On the way there we will recite the joyful mysteries of the rosary, and the sorrowful mysteries on returning. After breakfast at nine, we will make an Act of Adoration to the Sacred Heart, then each of us will have our individual duties until twelve thirty.

"After our morning work, we will go to our little chapel for an examination of conscience and a visit to the Blessed Sacrament. When Father Dubourg returns, he has promised to bring an altar, a tabernacle, and the Blessed Sacrament. He will sometimes say Mass for us here."

The announcement of Mass in their own house brought whispers of excitement.

"We will take turns reading a portion of the scripture while we eat dinner each night," Mother continued, "then we will have recreation. At two we will go again to the chapel to visit the Blessed Sacrament and read *The Imitation of Christ*. Then we will work until five, then return to the chapel to recite the glorious mysteries of the rosary and to make a longer visit to Jesus in the Blessed Sacrament.

During supper, we will read from *The Spiritual Combat* and have another time of recreation until eight-thirty. The day will end with reading from a spiritual book and night prayers together.

"How blessed it is to have such a regularity to our hours of the day!" Mother said, who was anxious for their life to begin in earnest. "Order is the thread which guides our actions in the labyrinth of time. Otherwise all runs to confusion."

Mother Seton's eyes sparkled as she looked at her eager sisters. "We must engrave this day on our hearts, July 31, 1809, for this day the Sisters of Charity are founded," she said. "How blessed are we to be the first native community of religious women in the United States!"

The sisters began their new life with enthusiasm and energy. Some worked in the house, others in the fields. They turned over the earth for a garden and planted vegetables. They bought cows, chickens, and lambs. Some pedaled at the spinning wheel, spinning wool into yarn. At recreation or in free moments, they all knit stockings for the Sulpicians' two seminaries to earn money for themselves. Mother Seton watched it all, overjoyed, reminding them, "Every good work we do is a grain of seed for eternal life."

Mother Seton thrived on the peaceful rhythm of her new life and always looked forward to Wednesdays, Seton family day, when her sons came to the Valley from Mount St. Mary's where they attended school. One Wednesday she and fourteen-year-old Anna, both with knitting needles clacking away, sat under a tree, chatting more like friends than mother and daughter and watching nine-year-old Kit and seven-year-old Rebecca play tag. The little dog a friend had given them raced from one to the other.

"Ma, is not God good to have brought us here? It is peaceful and the sisters take such good care of us. I could not find better companions anywhere." Anna leapt to her feet. "Will and Dick!" Anna ran after her two sisters to meet her brothers. They all hugged and, holding hands, ran toward their mother.

Tears welled up in Mother Seton's eyes. *I think my five cannot be surpassed for loveliness and sweetness of character,* she said to herself, watching them detour to Sister Kitty, who was picking raspberries at the edge of the garden.

Sister Kitty opened her arms wide as the boys ran to her and hugged her. She handed round a bucket filled with berries, while Sister Mary Ann and Sister Maria put down their hoes and watched. Harriet and Cecilia, who had regained some strength from the mountain air, hurried from the Stone House when they heard the boys. And Sister Rose, followed by the house sisters, came out onto the porch with a picnic basket.

"What a treat it is when the boys come!" Sister Susan exclaimed.

The children ran up to the porch, gave each sister a hug, and then ran to their mother whose eyes glistened with tears of gladness at the love between her children and the community.

Richard hugged his mother. "Ma, can we eat down by Toms Creek today?"

"Anna and I will carry the picnic basket, Ma." William took the basket from Sister Rose and gave Anna one of the handles.

They walked through the meadows. The three youngest, with the dog at their heels, raced one another to the creek.

Sounding very grown up, William reported, "Ma, this week during catechism class, Father asked if my business in the world would be to make money and gain a reputation or to serve God and make every endeavor to please him."

"And what did you answer?" Mother Seton stifled a smile.

"That my business was to do both, of course." William and Anna set the basket down under a tree next to the creek. "Oh Ma, I read about a boy whistling as he worked atop the sails of his ship. That's the life for me, I thought. I'll rove the world and see it all."

"Not me," said Richard who had walked up and was helping Anna spread the quilt. "I'll stay in the valley near Ma. It's a farmer's life for me."

The little family sat on the quilt, thanked God they could all be together again, and ate their lunch.

Mother finished her apple, then said, "Mr. Filicchi says in his last letter that all of his business ventures are successful because of our sisters' prayers and good works. But we would have no good works if it were not for his generosity. He has sent more money for the building of our new log house and says I must speak my wants to him as his sister. He reminds us to trust the One who clothes and feeds the birds of the air."

Anna reached for a piece of cheese. "Ma, tell them about Aunt Julia Scott's letter."

"Aunt Scott has sent Anna enough money to take art lessons in Baltimore next year. And Anna says the remainder goes to our clothing fund."

"When you write, Ma, do tell him that Sister Cecilia O'Conway is teaching me French, Spanish, and Italian. Perhaps I will write to him in Italian one day."

ELIZABETH ANN SETON

Eleven-year-old Richard handed his mother a cool drink from the stream and watched lovingly as she drank it. "Ma, God does take care of us, like Mr. Filicchi says. And Ma, can we go swimming?" Anticipating her yes, Richard began taking off his shoes.

Happily, Mother Seton watched her precious five swim, gather wildflowers, skip, and play with the lambs and the dog. She thought, *Sweet is the Providence that rules over us!*

CHAPTER TWELVE
TROUBLED ON EVERY SIDE

At recreation time one afternoon, after the sisters had helped themselves to some apples, Mother Seton said matter-of-factly, "Dear Ones, we are here on earth to work for our dear eternity. We know that death is our certain portion, and it would not do to be unprepared. We prepare spiritually, of course, each day, but the Adored would have us prepare a place to commit our bodies to the earth. It's a beautiful day! Let's walk around the farm and find a place for our eternal rest."

The sisters walked through the meadows, then Sister Rose pointed to a place in the woods. "Mother, look at this little wood. It has large grassy places where we could be buried."

"Yes," Mother agreed, "I like the idea that we would be able to see it from the new house."

Harriet tossed her apple core against a large oak tree and laughed, "I will rest under the oak tree just where the core has fallen."

When Mother Seton returned to her desk, she read a note from Father Dubourg saying they should no longer write Father Babade for spiritual direction. Mother was shocked. *Father Babade knows my soul,* she thought. *I am able to open myself to him as to no one else, and he helps me understand my newfound faith.* She rested her head in her hands. She had so little understanding of rules for religious communities, but to be cut off from his instruction, which was so necessary for someone in her position, with sisters to care for, seemed so severe a regulation!

After the evening rosary, Mother told the sisters that they must cease to write to Father Babade as their spiritual director. She expected Father Dubourg to take his place, or someone else equally competent.

The sisters gasped; several began to cry. The next day the sisters, usually lively and merry, worked without speaking. Their silence made Mother feel keenly her duty to these dear young women whose spiritual life she was responsible for. One by one during the course of the day, the sisters came to her.

"Oh, Mother," Sister Maria said, "Father Babade leads me straight to God. Please ask Father Dubourg to reconsider."

Sister Susan was angry. "Surely our Superior is acting like a tyrant, Mother. Do write Bishop Carroll. He is a father to us and will not deny your request."

Mother prayed for several days, then wrote Bishop Carroll explaining everything to him. Her letter ended: "I am accustomed to sacrifice what I most value in life, but my heart is torn when I see my sisters cannot bear this trial in the same way."

On Father Dubourg's next visit, he showed Mother Seton a copy of the temporary rules. "You see, the rule permits writing to a director only once every two months. And on designated subjects," he said testily. "I have also brought you a book on spiritual direction. I hope this will better help you understand the function of spiritual direction in a community like yours. Now I will build the altar for you and install the Blessed Sacrament."

Soon after his visit, he resigned as their Superior. Mother was distressed. After all, it was Father Dubourg who had made possible her dream of religious life. She wrote and asked his forgiveness for writing to the bishop. Then she wrote Bishop Carroll, asking him to reinstate Father Dubourg and admitting, "The truth is, my dear Father in God, I've been made a Mother before I was ready. I should have offered this up to God at once and helped the sisters to do so as well."

In a return letter, the bishop was kind but firm. Father John David would now be their Superior. Mother Seton placed the letter on her desk, slipped to her knees, bowed her head, and prayed for the strength to accommodate herself to this new situation: *Oh, my God, forgive what I have been, correct what I am, and direct what I shall be. Help me get rid of my self-will and to learn obedience.*

Before Father David arrived he wrote Mother, telling her his plans for the school and ordering her to make strict regulations for the community. Mother was vexed by his long-distance commands made without consulting the views of the community. For months she tried to bend her will to his but she could not, nor could she be completely open with him. She even questioned whether she should remain in her post. Again, she wrote the newly-elevated Archbishop Carroll who assured her that the ultimate success of the community depended on her continuing as Mother.

In the midst of her trouble with her superiors, her son William became seriously ill. Mother had him brought to her house and nursed him day and night, while everyone prayed. He continued to worsen until finally he was given the last sacraments and his aunt Harriet made a shroud.

Mother cried out to God, "Please, Lord, not my little Willy." She added weakly, "But your will be done."

Miraculously Willy recovered.

But no sooner had he returned to school than Harriet, who had been complaining of a painful headache for several weeks, became ill and could not leave her bed. Three days before Christmas she died, and was buried in their "little sacred wood," under the oak tree just where her apple core had landed months earlier. The shroud she had made for William was used for her.

The first Christmas in Emmitsburg was a sad one. Added to their grief was the disappointment that the new house was not finished. With the arrival of two new postulants, the Stone House was not only cramped but cold, and snow sifted through cracks and covered the sisters' blankets as they slept. Soon many were ill, including Anna, and Cecilia showed signs of decline. Mother Seton herself began to run a fever and experience pains in the chest.

She prayed to know how to lift the spirits of her sisters. One morning after prayer she told them, "I have decided that a few of us should live in the new house, even though it is not finished. Sisters Sally, Maria, and Rose have agreed to go. If it is too cold, they can return."

On the night the three sisters moved into the new house, it stormed. The following morning they ran through mud and rain from the White House to the Stone House for morning prayer. But when they opened the door, everyone was asleep.

They awakened Mother Seton who asked sleepily, "Have we overslept?"

"Oh dear," said Sister Rose, looking at the clock. "I woke up and thought surely it was time for morning prayer and woke the others."

They began to laugh, then Mother put a finger to her lips so they wouldn't wake the sleepers on the floor at her feet. "We did not make allowance for having one timepiece," she whispered. "We will have to come up with a plan. For the time being you can be relieved of morning prayer. Go back to sleep, although I hate sending you back into that sea of mud."

Muddied, too, and confused was the state of their fledgling community. Tension continued in her relationship with Father David. He wanted to send Mother Seton to Baltimore to start a school and make Rose White Mother Superior. Some priest advisors wanted Mother Seton to stay at Emmitsburg with Sister Rose as Mother Superior. Others wanted to send Sister Rose to Baltimore to start a hospital. Still others wanted a sister from France to come to America and be the new community's Mother Superior.

Mother Seton begged to know the Lord's will. She knelt before the tabernacle. How could she remain as Mother? Father David wanted to replace her, yet the French rule had no provision for a mother with five children to head a community. If a sister from France became head, what authority would she have over the Seton children? Should Mother Seton leave, find a teaching post, and care for her children? Or stay and see this all as a trial? Was this trial God's voice telling her to leave?

Mother rested her head on her folded hands and prayed. Then she picked up a spiritual book, opened it and read a story about St. Peter, whose disciples urged him to leave Rome when the persecution against the Christians broke out under Nero. Peter escaped by night, but going out of the city he met Jesus in a vision. St. Peter asked him, "Lord, where are you going?" Christ answered, "I am going to Rome to be crucified again." Peter went back to the city and stayed and suffered martyrdom.

Tears trickled down Mother's cheeks. "I shall stay as I am until the Adored's will be known," she decided.

That night she wrote in her journal: "I am sick, but not dying; troubled on every side, but not distressed; perplexed, but not despairing; afflicted, but not forsaken; cast down but not destroyed; knowing the affliction of this life is but for a moment, while the glory in the life to come will be eternal."

The uncertain state of the community brought on a kind of melancholy in the sisters, so Mother decided to move everyone to the new White House even though workmen were not finished and the first pupils were not to be admitted till the following week. The opportunity to channel the sisters' physical energy seemed to make them brighten, and soon everyone had a job packing up.

On February 20, 1810, Father Dubois, the mountain priest who had met them that first day, carried the Blessed Sacrament in procession from the Stone House to the chapel in what they called the White House. Cecilia was carried on a litter because she was so ill.

In the White House, Mother, who always thrived on activity and difficult circumstances, seemed to be everywhere at once. She superintended the school, which they called St. Joseph's, accepted new candidates, instructed all the country children in religion, taught the sisters how to teach the children, dealt with the confusion of rules and her status in the community, while keeping up the spirits of the sisters with her laughter and sense of humor. She also nursed her beloved young sister-in-law, Cecilia, who was in the last stages of tuberculosis. Both the doctor and Archbishop Carroll suggested that Mother Seton take her to Baltimore for more specialized medical treatment. But no treatment could help her. She died in Baltimore shortly after Easter and was buried back in Emmitsburg next to Harriet.

Shortly after Cecilia's death, Father David arrived with three candidates and the news that Napoleon would not grant the French sisters passports to America. Instead, a priest would bring the French rule, which would take a few months to translate from the French into English. Father David exacted strict discipline the few months he was Superior, but then he was transferred to Kentucky, and Mother's dear wish that Father Dubois be their new Superior was granted. On one of his regular visits, Father Dubois brought Father Simon Bruté who had just arrived from France.

"Hello, Mother, I make English very bad," Father Bruté said.

Mother welcomed him in fluent French, thankful once again that her father had insisted on her faithfulness to learning it.

Father Bruté was delighted to hear her and spoke in his native French, "I try to force this dreadful English into my backward head so I can preach when I go out to the missions."

"Mother," asked Father Dubois, "would you teach the English to Father Bruté? You speak French so well."

Several times a week Mother Seton and Father Bruté translated *The Imitation of Christ*. Her soul burst into flame for love of God as they talked in English about what they had translated. She found a soul who understood hers and it soared heavenward. She said to herself, "Father Bruté must be the angel guardian promised me at Gibraltar."

Within a few months Father Bruté was sent on mission to Baltimore but his frequent letters ignited her soul and left her smiling at the clumsy English.

When the English translation of the French rules finally arrived, the sisters discussed them and made a few modifications. Mother Seton would remain as Mother Superior and keep her five children with her. They also recommended including education of the young as a purpose of their community and that they be allowed to take in boarders, since they were in a newly formed country that was mostly Protestant.

After the final unanimous vote, Mother sent the rules to Archbishop Carroll with a letter saying that the proposed changes kept the rules close to the original ones sent from France. Mother Seton hoped that, in approving the changes, he would remember the many difficulties she had faced over time and that her first duty must always be to her own children. She mailed the letter, praying that she and her community could soon take their vows as Sisters of Charity.

CHAPTER THIRTEEN
PREPARING GOOD LEAVEN

Mother Seton smiled with affection at her class of older girls. Her goal in teaching was not to turn them into nuns, but to send them back into their place in society. As good wives and mothers, they would be leaven to the world. And yet, if one of them wished to become a Sister of Charity, that girl would find herself both fortunate and happy.

"Today we will talk about virtue," Mother Seton said. "We must consider beauty but a superficial grace. Beauty should be used to attract others to virtue. When we think only of our exterior loveliness and admiring glances we can become vain, and perhaps deface and disfigure the image of God in our souls. When we clothe this cherished gift, we must avoid all extravagance in dress on the one hand and carelessness on the other."

Mother spoke to them as she would her daughters. "Let me tell you a story about dangerous amusements. A butterfly asked an owl, 'How can I go close to a candle without burning my wings?' The owl counseled her, 'Do not even look at the smoke.'" Mother looked at each of them with kindness. "How can a soul belonging to God frequent places where purity is easily blemished? Must you first burn your little wings before you withdraw from the flame?

It is easier to keep away from such pleasures than to try to use them well," she exhorted them gently.

Afterwards, Mother could hear the angelic voices of the music class as she walked through the hall toward a workman. "Will the house be finished before the winter rains?" she asked.

"Only if the weather holds, Mother," he replied.

Farther down the hall she met Father Dubois, who had come to teach a religion class. They walked into the class together. Mother stood in the back listening to Father Dubois instruct the children in his heavy French accent. Speaking of how they must enliven one another's faith, he said, "You must be like so many stumps of fire." He hesitated a moment, considering his words. "Hmmm. Stumps of fire?" He looked at Mother questioningly. "No, chunks of fire!" he continued enthusiastically. "You must be like chunks of fire, put together make a great fire; one, if left alone, soon goes out."

Mother almost laughed out loud and thought with tenderness, *I'm an old black stump that would soon go out without the live coal of Father Dubois' spirit to set me ablaze.*

When the pupils had left, he said, "Mother, I have good news for you. Father Bruté is coming to reside again at Mount St. Mary's. If you agree, we would like him to be your spiritual director."

Mother clasped her hands together. "Nothing could give me more joy, Father. With you as my Superior and Father Bruté as my Spiritual Director, I should speed on my way to God."

Lighthearted at the news, Mother looked in on the student workroom. The spinning wheels' whir and the clack of knitting needles were like background music for Sister

Rose's quiet instruction. Some students cut out clothes, some mended students' clothing, others practiced fancy embroidery stitches, and one was learning to weave cloth.

Mother returned to her desk and just picked up her pen when Sister Rose came to the door. "Mother, I fear I disturb you too often."

"Not at all. The sunbeams are not more welcome through my windows than your well-known step at my door." She replaced her pen in the inkhorn.

"I overheard a conversation between Mary Harper and Clotilde Brawner which I thought you would want to know about." Sister Rose closed the door. "Mary asked Clotilde in a haughty, self-important tone, 'Do you know who I am?' When Clotilde replied, 'No,' Mary said, 'Well, I am General Robert Goodloe Harper's daughter.'"

"Oh dear," Mother replied, displeased. "Perhaps we must remind Mary of her true parentage. She might be a more agreeable companion."

Mother found Mary and asked her to walk with her to the chapel. Gently she asked the girl, "Mary, is it not God who has made you?"

"Yes, Mother."

"And he made Clotilde as well?" Mother opened the chapel door.

"Yes, Mother." Mary's tone hinted at impatience.

"And who died on the cross for your sins?" asked Mother, standing in front of her beloved picture of the Redeemer.

"Jesus," said Mary, a little subdued.

"And he died for Clotilde as well. Is that true?"

"Yes, Mother."

"I wonder who he loves more, you or Clotilde," Mother said.

"He loves us both the same, I would suppose," Mary answered.

"As you sit here looking at our Blessed Redeemer, think about how God loves Clotilde and your other companions with the same love as he loves you. You are spiritual sisters. You all came from God, and your destiny is eternal life. When you hear the bell ring for drawing, you may join your class, dear," she said with as much sternness as she could muster.

The bell sounded for recreation and she watched her "merry fry" pour from the school. *I cannot stay away from the children when I hear their laughter,* she thought. *Lord, this is what I was born for.* She went outside and the children gathered around her like bees around a honeycomb.

"Mother, our father is going to church and to the sacraments after his visit with you," said one of the girls. "He has said to our friends in New York that he would travel across the land just to get a glimpse of your eyes."

Mother put her head back and laughed, "It must be the peace of Jesus that attracts him, don't you think?" Mother tousled the girl's hair. "Do you remember I asked you to pray for Mrs. Sadler, a friend of mine, whom I had never talked to about religion? I learned today she has become a Catholic."

She patted another girl's cheek. "And now I must not play the truant any longer. I must get back to work and so must you."

The girls were divided into groups of ten students, called a decury, which had an experienced pupil set over each to aid them in their studies and spiritual progress. Mother Seton's three daughters headed decuries, and she stopped a moment to watch them. Thirteen-year-old Kit was listening to her girls' lessons. Bec's ten were poor children from the countryside. And there was Anna, her dearest Anna, speaking softly to her own group.

Mother's heart welled up with love for her seventeen-year-old daughter, followed by an icy dagger of fear. Anna had complained of breathing problems and pains in the chest since being caught in a September rain. Even now Mother noticed a lingering dry cough and she feared tuberculosis. She wondered if Anna's desire to become a Sister of Charity would be fulfilled.

At the end of the year, Mother leafed through a pile of bills. Because Napoleon Bonaparte had sealed off Europe, and hostilities between Britain and the United States were escalating, there had been a sharp rise in prices and a shortage of goods. There was no material for habits and the sisters were eating buttermilk soup and drinking carrot coffee. She knew that if she did not find financial assistance she would have to close the school, and the sisters would have to return to their homes. Neither did she have money to pay off her personal bills. Antonio had always helped in the past, but with Europe cut off from all shipping she could not send or receive letters. She looked up at Christ on the cross. "Whom should I go to for help?"

The answer came at once. She wrote General Harper, who had helped them financially before. She also wrote her dear friend, Julia, and it was to Julia that Mother Seton confessed her personal needs and fears. Not only did Anna have all the symptoms of tuberculosis, but her youngest daughter Rebecca had slipped on the ice and had told no one because Anna was already sick. Now Bec was in pain and walked with a limp and a doctor said her condition could not be helped. Yet Mother Seton was happy, she wrote to Julia, although her happiness was only the result of grace.

CHAPTER FOURTEEN
THE LITTLE MUSTARD SEED

Mother's heart was breaking as she wrote again to Julia and shared the terrible news: Anna died from tuberculosis on March 12, 1812. At least her daughter had been able to take her vows for the first time just a few days before and so had died a Sister of Charity. Mother Seton's grief threatened to overwhelm her. If she had not had her other children and her community to care for, she would rather have died herself to be with her daughter.

After Anna's death, Mother went about her duties with charity and sweetness on the exterior, while her soul remained in anguish. Month after month, Father Bruté urged her to abandon herself to the will of God. He exhorted her to hope, but he could not rouse her desolate soul. Then, six months after Anna's death, Father Bruté urged, "Mother, let us be courageous and accept with love and zeal the will and order of Providence. Let us not refuse to live. The longest life is nothing to eternity, and yet the most generous saints desired to remain."

His words plucked a string in her heart. "The most generous saints desired to remain," she repeated to herself. "The longest life is nothing to eternity." Little by little, under Father Bruté's direction, Mother Seton's dry and weary spirit revived, her trials eased, and once again she began to go about her day with a joyful spirit to match her joyful exterior.

Among Mother's duties was teaching the sisters and instructing the children. She would walk to the front of the chapel filled with joy at the sight of her "white caps" and "black caps," the children and the sisters, kneeling in prayer. She knelt before her Adored in the tabernacle, bent her head and prayed, then stood before them.

"Our meditation today will be about our daily work," she began one lesson. "I will tell you what is a great help to me. The first rule of our dear Savior's life was to do his Father's will. The aim of each day for us also is to do God's will. Secondly, to do it in the manner he wills, and thirdly to do it because it *is* his will. That is how he lives in me and how I live in union with him every minute of the day.

"I know *what* his will is by those who direct my work; whatever they bid me do, no matter how small in itself, is the will of God for me. I try to do it in a pleasing manner, that is, not rushing because I am hurried or being watched, not creeping like a snail because no one pushes me. Finally, I must be ready to quit at any moment to do anything else to which I may be called by those over me."

As Mother talked, Sam—her name for the devil—whispered in her ear: "See how they are affected! How silent and attentive! What respect! What looks of love!"

Mother thought: *Oh Adored! See how Sam tries to distract me. Oh my soul, do not even look toward him, but keep on speaking with your eyes on our Dearest.* Still, her heart was heavy because of the temptation. Later, she felt unworthy to receive communion, but there sprang to her mind the comforting image of the Lord as a shepherd, caring even for the likes of her.

ELIZABETH ANN SETON

Despite their financial problems, the sisters were able to stay in the valley and keep their school open because of the generosity of General Harper and his wealthy friends, who sent their daughters to Saint Joseph's Academy. The sisters also decreased their spending, gave up sugar and other niceties, and earned money by sewing vests, pants, and coats for the priests at the Mount. One night, eating her buttermilk soup and bread and eating also the bread crusts of the elderly sister next to her who could not chew, Mother suddenly remembered her plentiful dining room table as a young married woman in her own beautiful home. Tears began but she heard the good Lord say to her, *Look up! If you had your little morsel alone, of better quality, no pains of body or reluctance to eat, what part would I have in your meal? For you to be here in your place, to keep order, give example, eat cheerfully the little you have, in the spirit of love as if before my tabernacle is all I ask. I will do the rest. Abandon all. Abandon all.*

Abandon all she did—including her desire for the sisters to take their vows as an American community. For more than two years, they had been living according to the rules of the Daughters of Charity of St. Vincent De Paul. Then, finally, the long-looked-for day arrived. On July 19, 1813, eighteen sisters pronounced their vows of poverty, chastity, obedience, and service to the poor. The first American community of the Sisters of Charity was a reality! For this special meditation, Mother Seton wrote, "Let us keep in mind our detachment from earth, our humility, our poverty, our chastity, our love, our courage in trials, our zeal in duties, our charity to all, be it all in all to us."

Several months later, at recreation outside on the grass, Sister Margaret said, "We are buried in the midst of woods and valleys! Nobody knows what we are doing. Truly the world forgets us."

Sister Rose answered her, "Do not grieve so much; depend on it, this valley, quiet as it is, will give such a roar someday that the noise will sound all over America."

In the summer of 1814, Mother Seton opened a letter from Father Hurley of Philadelphia requesting sisters to come and manage an orphanage for children whose parents had died of yellow fever. Mother closed her eyes and lifted her face to heaven. "O Beloved!" she said aloud, "Perhaps our little mustard seed begins to grow."

The little mustard seed of the Sisters of Charity received more requests to open establishments or take over existing ones. When she received a request from New York City, Mother Seton said aloud, "Oh my! What a different turn events have taken. I wonder what my relatives and friends will say? They will certainly scrutinize our work closely, knowing that I'm the Mother." She laid the letter on her desk. "Whom shall I send?"

The answer was clear. She should ask Sister Rose, who was heading the Philadelphia orphanage, and Sisters Cecilia O'Conway and Felicitas Brady should assist her.

The night before their departure, just as she was climbing into bed, Mother heard a light tap on her door. It was Cecilia. After apologizing for the hour, she said, "Mother, you know for some time I have had such a desire to live a contemplative life. How can I pray amid so many duties and children? Mother, am I really the one to send?"

"Dear Cis, this sounds like Sam is tempting you. Remember why you are going on this heavenly errand. To crucify self! The needs of the United States demand other vocations besides the contemplative one. This is not a country, my dear one, for solitude and silence, but a country of warfare and crucifixion. We must look to the Kingdom of Souls. There are so few to work in the little vineyard. I know it is difficult to live among so many chattering children all day long, yet this is what God expects of us. And we must look after their souls as well as our own."

Mother rose, hugged Cecilia to her, then held her at arm's length. "Love our Mother above," she advised. "She will comfort you. I do not feel the least uneasiness about you. If you suffer, so much the better for our high journey above. The only fear I have is that you will let the old string pull too hard for solitude and silence."

"Thank you, Mother. I know you're right." Comforted, Sister Cecilia went to bed.

She and the others left the next morning—June 20, 1817. Mother watched their carriage until it was a speck in the distance, thinking, *I seem always to be saying goodbye to my dear ones.* She sent a prayer aloft for her children.

One night in September, Mother woke with a start. *Lord,* she said to herself, *is it William's angel who woke me? Please bless William. How many twists and turns to Divine Providence, with William, Richard, and dearest Bec all in new vocations.*

William had gone to Leghorn to learn the shipping business from Antonio Filicchi, but he'd had no aptitude for business. He then returned to the United States and joined the Navy, his desire since childhood. Richard, after graduation from Mount St. Mary's, tried a few accounting positions then took William's place with the Filicchis.

Mother looked out at the moon shining full on the "little sacred wood" with its white crosses. She looked at the bittersweet sight twenty times a day. Since last year, Bec had a new vocation as well. After her fall on the ice several years ago, she had developed a tumor on her leg. Now she was buried close to Anna. Mother thought: *Dear, dear Rebecca! I have lost the little friend of my heart, who read every pain or joy of it. You soothed my every daily care, dear darling of my soul.*

Now Mother had only lovely Kit with her. But Kit needed some experience of the world outside the simple life of Emmitsburg. Mother had hoped Kit might have a religious vocation, but it didn't seem to be God's will for her. Mother decided to send her to friends in Baltimore to study music and drawing, then to Julia in Philadelphia. Afterwards, Eliza Sadler and relatives in New York would give Kit an opportunity to see another side of things.

Getting out of bed, Mother lit a candle and smelled the bouquet of white violets in a tumbler on the desk next to her half-knitted stocking. She picked up the map she kept on the desk to feel close to William, kissed it, and prayed: *Dear Lord, keep my William safe wherever he is on these vast seas of yours.* She wrote advice to Kit in a little red leather pocket-size journal, sent a prayer on high for her children, and went back to bed, sighing from the pain of an abscess on her breast.

When Kit returned from her travels to Philadelphia and New York, Mother was recuperating from a serious inflammation of the lungs. She laced her arm through her daughter's and they walked slowly to the barn to look at the newborn calves.

"Mother, we have had a good life here!" Kit helped Mother sit down on a stump by the barnyard. "You don't know what a difference it was being away from you, having no mother to consult, and so many things I wanted to talk with you about first. How I missed you." Kit picked up a small gray kitten and handed it to her. "I read and reread the red journal you gave me ever so many times—and felt closer to you."

Mother petted the kitten lying on her lap, with its eyes closed to the sun, and looked out at the meadows. "Look at all the lambs. They outnumber the sheep, just as our schoolchildren outnumber their teachers. There are seventy-two boarders now, eighteen vowed sisters, sixteen novices, and two candidates. We prepare them like good seed to be scattered throughout America. And just as many more would join us if we had the room."

Kit sat down on the grass next to her mother. "The sisters in New York are well regarded by our friends and relatives. Mrs. Sadler is especially pleased by their good reputation."

Mother slipped the kitten from her lap and held up her hand so Kit could help her to her feet. "Dear Kit, General Harper wrote not long ago. He knows the condition of my health and has offered you their home when I go to our dear eternity. The family is so fond of you. I do believe it will be the best situation for you. The good God has let me see two daughters safely to eternity and to raise my sons, and now, if I knew that you were cared for, I would be at ease."

"You know how I love the Harper family. The girls are like sisters to me. If I cannot live here with you, I would be well pleased to live with the Harpers," Kit said, yet her eyes filled with tears as she spoke and she hugged Mother to her.

"Peace, my soul's darling. Look up at the blue heaven and love him. He is so good to us."

They walked slowly through the summer sun toward the house.

Mother kept up with as many of her duties as her declining health allowed. She received requests for sisters to open orphanages and schools in Philadelphia and Baltimore, although no new missions were actually begun before 1821. No sooner did she send one group of sisters out than others replaced them as candidates. The Sisters of Charity opened free schools and tuition-paying schools with most of their orphanages. The number of students at St. Joseph's increased as well and, as Mother began her third term, Father Dubois began building a new school for day students from the countryside.

The little mustard seed had grown into a tree and was extending its branches.

CHAPTER FIFTEEN
ROAR FROM THE VALLEY

One golden day in October Mother walked slowly through the meadow, then sat on a rock and looked around at the trees painted every shade of red and yellow. "How wonderful are your works," she said aloud. Her soul adored and praised God, and she cried out, "O God! O God! Give Yourself. What is all the rest?"

The Lord's voice of love answered, "I am yours."

Then her soul was silent before the divine Majesty, the silence that is the highest praise, the silence which proceeds from contemplating his perfections and greatness, the silence that desires only to be conformed to his will and sacrificed wholly to him.

A familiar voice behind her called her name. When she turned, William, in his white midshipman's uniform, hat in hand, was running toward her. With tears, they clung to one another, unable to speak a word. Finally, William let her go and sat her on the rock. Sitting at her feet, he took her hand.

"Ma, I am certain now God hears your prayers for my safety," he said. "September 18 our frigate left Boston for Chile, but off the coast of Virginia she ran into storms. I dreamt you stood by me, asking sorrowfully, 'Are you prepared?' Then I sprang from my hammock and the water reached my knees. The damage was so serious we pulled into Norfolk for repairs. I walked and begged rides from there."

Tears streamed down her face as she remembered the night last month when she was startled awake from her sleep. William became a golden blur in a golden day. When she could speak again, she said, "Thank you, God. Thank you, Willy's good angel. Thank you for delivering my Willy from evil."

William's visit cheered her and distracted her from the suffering of inflamed lungs and the ulcer on her breast. She wrote to Antonio about William's visit and ended: "Death has been grinning at me and threatening *his* visit as well. But I look forward to joining my loved ones and our dear Bishop Carroll."

Mother continued to get weaker and had to stay in bed. One day Father Bruté's familiar knock sounded on the door. "So," he said cheerfully, "you think you are going to plunge into the blessed abyss?"

"I cannot die to myself, and so I try to die the other way. Still, I try to keep the straight path to God alone. My daily lesson is to keep quietly in his presence." She pointed toward the partition that separated her room from the chapel. "I make my breathing a thanksgiving."

Father sat next to her bed. "So you will gather a little more of the florets of our valleys for your crown."

"I'm learning that the florets of the low valleys for the infirm are meekness, patience, resignation, and gratitude for help received." She looked past him out the window at a pale sun. "And I ask myself, am I in full charity toward all?"

Father patted her hand. "Yes, my child of heaven. Keep humility, simplicity, and charity. These will carry us through to eternity."

As Father left, Kit walked in, picked up a bottle of port, poured a glass, and handed it to Mother.

"The doctor's orders, I am afraid, are much too pleasing to this old carcass." Mother sipped the port. "We must write Aunt Scott. She is so faithful in supporting us and our little mustard seed."

Kit, who now handled all Mother's correspondence, sat down at her desk, smiling as she took up the stub of pen everyone teased Mother about.

"What are you doing, darling?" Mother dictated cheerfully. "I see bills from the sisters in Philadelphia paid by Julia Scott. The Lord will reward one who is so generous to support so poor an establishment as ours. If I was not convinced that your offering is a thousand-fold value to your dear soul, I would feel a real pain in it. William will be out of the service in January. He is now off the coast of Panama. Dick is coming home from Italy soon. He has not the ability or will for business and goes into the Navy. Dear Sad is off to France."

A cloud momentarily crossed Mother's face when she realized she would not see Julia or Sad again in this life. Then Sister Susan opened the door and said, "Mother, I have a surprise. One of your former pupils is here to visit you."

Mother opened her arms to Ella, who flew across the room.

"Mother, I heard you were ill. I'm leaving for France with my new husband, but I couldn't go without saying goodbye."

Mother and Ella embraced with tears for a long moment, then she sat on the edge of the bed holding Mother's hand.

"Tell me about your husband, dear," Mother said, her spirits raised by Ella's presence.

"Mother, he is wonderful. He is not handsome but he has a good character and he loves God. He is in his father's tailoring business. We hope to look at cloth while we are in France."

"Your French will be put to good use then. Remember how you cried over masculine and feminine endings?"

Mother and Ella exchanged memories, until Mother lay back wearily on her pillow.

"I've stayed much too long," Ella said. "Would you give me your blessing before I leave?"

Mother raised her hand over Ella, saying, "God bless you, my loved child. Remember Mother's first lesson to you: 'Seek God in all things.' In all your actions submit your motives to this unerring test: Will this give glory to God?"

She held Ella's hands and said, "You will never see Mother again on this earth. May we meet in heaven. The wheels of this old carriage are broken down, but then with the wings of a dove will my soul fly and be at rest. Remember me, and if you love poor old Mother, pray for her."

With tears streaming down her face, Ella kissed her and ran from the room.

One afternoon Mother asked Sister Margaret, "How are the children? I regret that I cannot visit them, but I thank God you have a mother's heart for them."

"Would you like to see them? If you cannot go to them, they will come to visit you."

"But they might be frightened to see me so ill."

"We will help you sit up, Mother, and you will have for them a cheerful face. It will be good for the children, and for you, too."

The following day Mother Seton sat up in bed while the children filed in, class by class, many of the girls with bouquets. Soon bunches of white violets, yellow cowslips and lilacs, and branches of apple, mock orange, and dogwood

blossoms covered her bed. She said to the girls after she blessed them, "Love the church. God's greatest gift to me was to come into the Catholic Church. Be children of the church. Stay in her care. Then will I be at peace about you."

Daily Mother grew weaker. She could no longer direct affairs from her bed and Sister Mary Xavier temporarily took her place. Then one cool day in late summer, she felt well enough to visit the building site of the new school and followed Father Dubois out among the carpenters.

"Mother," Father said, leading the way up the planks, "we believe our Lord says to continue to build. Never mind the trouble of banks or rumors of war with Spain. He takes care of that."

Mother climbed onto a pile of boards to better see the progress. An icy wind bit through her shawl into her breast. A few days later she developed a high fever and everyone thought the end was near. But after Father Dubois gave her extreme unction, she rallied and dictated a letter to Antonio about the community's activities. As for herself, she wrote, her soon-expected death would be as routine as housework.

Mother lost so much weight the sisters brought in a feather mattress to ease her pain. At night her lips were parched and dry from her illness. One night when Sister Anastasia, who had been Mother's housekeeper in Baltimore, brought her a drink, Mother said, "Forget the drink, or I would not be able to receive our blessed Lord. One communion more perhaps."

Sister Mary Xavier came into the room and felt Mother's hot forehead. "How are you doing, Mother?"

"I do not suffer. I am weak, it is true, but how happily and quietly the day passes!" Mother's large brown eyes were bright with fever. "If this be the way of death, nothing can be more peaceful and happy, and if I am to recover, still how sweet to rest in the arms of our Lord."

Sister Mary Xavier wiped the perspiration from Mother's forehead with a cool, damp cloth.

"I never felt more aware of the presence of our Dearest than since I have been sick," Mother Seton said with closed eyes and a smile on her lips. "It seems as if Our Lord or his Blessed Mother stood continually by me in bodily form, to comfort, cheer, and encourage me in the weary and tedious hours of pain." She took Sister Mary Xavier's hand and kissed it. "You will laugh at my imaginations. Still our All has many ways of comforting his little atoms."

When Sister Margaret came in to check on her, Mother said, "Margaret, did the children have enough to eat for supper tonight? Give them my portion. I don't need it any longer."

"Yes, Mother. They've eaten well. And there is enough for you besides."

In the morning Father Bruté came to give Mother holy communion. As he placed the ciborium upon the little table Mother burst into tears and, sobbing aloud, covered her face with her two hands.

"Be still, Mother! Peace, peace to you! Here is the Lord of peace! Have you any pain? Do you wish to confess?"

"No. Only give him to me," she said, her voice filled with longing and love.

"Peace, dear Mother, receive with great peace your God of peace."

Mother received her Adored and was lost in contemplation.

On January 2, with all the sisters kneeling around her bed and Kit close to her mother's head, Father Dubois administered extreme unction once again.

Mother whispered, "Very thankful." Then she lifted up her faint voice and said with a heaving breast, "I am thankful, Sisters, for your kindness to be present at this trial. Be children of the church. Be children of the church!"

On January 4, 1821, at one in the morning, Sister Anastasia called Sister Mary Xavier and Kit. "Come quickly. I think Mother is dying."

Sister Mary Xavier placed her hand on Mother's head.

Mother whispered, "Well, Xavier? How are you, dear?"

"Mother is suffering in the pit of her stomach," said Sister Anastasia.

Kit knelt down close to the head of the bed.

"Nothing to be done," said Mother weakly.

Sister Mary Xavier whispered, "Mother, our Lord is going to take you to himself."

Mother, her voice almost inaudible, said, "I adore."

Kit began to cry aloud and seemed almost in convulsions. Sister Cecilia helped her up and took her to the side.

A few moments later, Mother whispered the prayer of St. Pius VII, one of her favorite prayers: "May the most just, the most high, and the most amiable will of God be in all things fulfilled and praised and exalted above all forever."

Sister Mary Xavier knew Mother loved prayers in French and said the Gloria and Magnificat in French. She could feel the presence of the Lord waiting to receive Mother's soul.

Not long after midnight, Mother Seton ceased to breathe and she entered her dear eternity. The following day she was buried in her "little sacred wood" near her two daughters, her two sisters-in-law, and fifteen of her Sisters of Charity.

EPILOGUE

At the time of her death, Mother Seton was a pioneer in the Catholic Church in America. Her little mustard seed had grown to fifty sisters in Emmitsburg, New York City, Philadelphia, and Mount Saint Mary's. By 1850 there were foundations of sisters caring for orphanages, schools, and hospitals all over the United States. When Elizabeth Seton became a Catholic in 1805, there was one bishop in the United States. In 1820 there were six bishops and one archbishop.

Her daughter Catherine, or Kit, lived with the Harpers for a few years then traveled with William to Italy, England, and throughout America. She was the first novice to enter the New York Sisters of Mercy in 1846. For twenty-five years she visited the city prison and was beloved as a friend of prisoners. A burglar willed her a trunk containing pistols, jimmies, and other burglar tools, and a suit of clothing—all he owned in the world. She became Mother Assistant of her community and died April 3, 1891, at age 91.

Richard became captain's clerk and U.S. assistant agent at Monrovia. On the ship *Oswego* while nursing back to health a dying Episcopalian, the first American consul in Liberia, Richard contracted a fever. He died at sea on June 26, 1823.

William returned from the Pacific on June 19, 1821. Father Bruté gave him the unopened letter William had written to his mother which arrived after she had died. Father Bruté told William of his mother's holy death. Some years later, in 1845, William visited Emmitsburg and asked Mother Xavier Clark to erect a little chapel over his mother's grave. The chapel still stands today, built with the funds William contributed for the memorial for his beloved mother.

William resigned from the Navy and married Emily Prime on July 17, 1832. They had nine children. His son, Robert, became an archbishop in 1903. William died in New York, January 13, 1868, and is buried at Mount St. Mary's.

A half-nephew of Mother Seton became the first bishop of Newark and archbishop of Baltimore. Archbishop James Roosevelt Bayley was also an ancestor of Franklin D. Roosevelt.

After Mother Seton's death, Father Bruté exhorted the sisters to gather up all the fragments of her writings and belongings. He said they would be very important for the future. His words were prophetic. On September 14, 1975, Pope Paul VI pronounced to some sixteen thousand Americans in St. Peter's Square in Rome, "Elizabeth Ann Bayley Seton is a saint." A roar rose from the crowd for this first United States-born saint—wife, mother of five children, convert, foundress of the Sisters of Charity, and pioneer educator of the American Catholic school system. Her feast day is celebrated on January 4.

NOTES

Certain selections throughout the book were closely para-
phrased or quoted in whole or in part from the following
sources:

Chapter Three

Elizabeth's notes to Will can be found in *Elizabeth Bayley*
Seton: Collected Writings. New York: New City Press,
2000.

Chapter Seven

Elizabeth's thoughts while hearing the Blessed Sacrament carried through the streets can be found in ASJPH
1-3-3-8:60. Used with permission. Courtesy of Archives,
Daughters of Charity (Emmitsburg).

Chapter Eight

Elizabeth's prayer at Will's grave can be found in AMSV
110:M,11,12. Used with permission. Courtesy of Archives,
Sisters of Charity of New York.

ELIZABETH ANN SETON

Elizabeth's plea for faith after meeting Reverend Hobart
and her prayer during her last attendance of an Episcopal
service can both be found in ASJPH 1–3–3–10:3a. Used
with permission. Courtesy of Archives, Daughters of Charity (Emmitsburg).

Chapter Eleven

Elizabeth's thoughts while watching her children swim
can be found in ASJPH 1–3–3–6:71. Used with permission. Courtesy of Archives, Daughters of Charity (Emmitsburg).

Chapter Twelve

Mother Seton's prayer for strength to accept her new
Superior can be found in ASCSII, the flyleaf of her copy of
The Imitation of Christ. Used with permission. Courtesy of
Archives, Sisters of Charity of Seton Hill (Greensburg).

Chapter Fourteen

Mother Seton hearing the Lord's voice comforting her at
dinner can be found in *Life of Mrs. E. A. Seton* by Charles
White, Baltimore, 1852, pp 408–409.

Mother Seton's thoughts on the death of her daughter
Rebecca can be found in ASJPH 1–3–3–9:21. Used with
permission. Courtesy of Archives, Daughters of Charity
(Emmitsburg).

Chapter Fifteen

Mother Seton's deathbed comments can be found in *Life of Mrs. E. A. Seton* by Charles White, Baltimore, 1852, page 423, and in ASJPH 1–3–3–12:3,3. Used with permission. Courtesy of Archives, Daughters of Charity (Emmitsburg).

SELECTED BIBLIOGRAPHY

Alderman, Margaret and Josephine Burns. *Praying with Elizabeth Seton*. Winona, Minn.: St. Mary's Press, 1992.

Bechtle, Regina, S.C. and Judith Metz, S.C., eds. *Elizabeth Bayley Seton: Collected Writings*. New York: New City Press, 2000.

Code, Msgr. Joseph B. *Letters of Mother Seton to Mrs. Julianna Scott*. Emmitsburg: Sisters of Charity of St. Vincent De Paul, 1928, 1960.

————. *Daily Thoughts of Mother Seton*. Emmitsburg: Mother Seton Guild, 1960.

Cuzzolina, Marie Celeste, S.C. *Elizabeth Ann Seton, A Self-Portrait*. Libertyville, Ill.: Franciscan Marytown Press, 1986.

————. *Intimate Friendships of Elizabeth Ann Bayley* Seton. New York: Alba House, 1989.

Dirvin, Joseph I., C.M. *Mrs. Seton, Foundress of American Sisters of Charity*. New York: Farrar, Straus and Giroux, 1962, 1975.

ELIZABETH ANN SETON

. *The Soul of Elizabeth Seton.* San Francisco: Ignatius Press, 1990.

Feeney, Leonard, S.J. *Mother Seton, An American Woman.* New York: Dodd, Mead Company, 1947.

Flanagan, Mary Kathleen, S.C. *The Influence of John Henry Hobart on the Life of Elizabeth Ann Seton.* Ann Arbor, Mich.: University Microfilms International, 1979.

Hoare, Mary Regis. *Virgin Soil.* Boston: The Christopher Publishing House, 1942.

Kelly, Ellin M. and Annabelle Melville eds. *Elizabeth Seton, Selected Writings.* New York/Mahwah: Paulist Press, 1987.

Melville, Annabelle M. *Elizabeth Bayley Seton.* New York: Charles Scribner's Sons, 1951.

Metz, Judith, S.C. *A Retreat with Elizabeth Seton: Meeting Our Grace.* Cincinnati: Saint Anthony Messenger Press, 1999.

Reville, John C., S.J. *The First American Sister of Charity.* New York: The America Press, 1921.

Seton, Robert Msgr., D.D. *Memoir, Letters and Journal of Elizabeth Seton,* 2 vols. New York: P. O. Shea Publishers, 1869.

White, Charles I. *Life of Mrs. E. A. Seton* (Baltimore: 1852), revised as *Mother Seton, Mother of Many Daughters.* New York: Doubleday, 1949.